OUR BROKEN Hallelujahs

REBECCA BURTRAM

WESTBOW
PRESS®
A DIVISION OF THOMAS NELSON
& ZONDERVAN

All the stories in this book are true. However, some names have been changed in order to respect the privacy of the individuals involved in the circumstances.

Scriptures marked as "(CEV)" are taken from the Contemporary English Version Copyright © 1995 by American Bible Society. Used by permission.

Scripture quotations marked NLT are taken from the Holy Bible, New Living Translation, copyright © 1996, 2004, 2007. Used by permission of Tyndale House Publishers, Inc. Carol Stream, Illinois 60188. All rights reserved. Website

Scripture quotations marked NIV are taken from the Holy Bible, New International Version®. NIV®. Copyright © 1973, 1978, 1984 by International Bible Society. Used by permission of Zondervan. All rights reserved.

WestBow Press books may be ordered through booksellers or by contacting:

WestBow Press
A Division of Thomas Nelson & Zondervan
1663 Liberty Drive
Bloomington, IN 47403
www.westbowpress.com
1 (866) 928-1240

ISBN: 978-1-5127-7124-4 (sc)
ISBN: 978-1-5127-7126-8 (hc)
ISBN: 978-1-5127-7125-1 (e)

Library of Congress Control Number: 2017900285

Print information available on the last page.

WestBow Press rev. date: 1/30/2017

Contents

INTRODUCTION
WHEN HALLELUJAH WON'T COME VII

PART 1
THE UNSPEAKABLE ACTS OF OTHERS

Chapter 1   My First Wound 1
Chapter 2   Emma's Broken Hallelujah.................................. 15
Chapter 3   God's Love is Unfailing 21

PART 2
THE BROKENNESS OF LIVING

Chapter 4   The Breaking That Followed 29
Chapter 5   Brooke's Broken Hallelujah.................................41
Chapter 6   God's Love is Present 47

PART 3
A DESPERATE NEED FOR GRACE

Chapter 7   The Damage I Had Done 55
Chapter 8   Tamara's Broken Hallelujah 69
Chapter 9   God's Unconditional Love 77

CONCLUSION
WHAT GOOD IS A BROKEN HALLELUJAH?

Chapter 10 God's Love Redeems the Brokenness 85
Chapter 11 Kristi's Broken Hallelujah.................................93
About the Book...100
About the Author 102
Study Plans 103

Introduction

WHEN HALLELUJAH WON'T COME

Let's sing together, or not. Maybe the singing is too hard because the pain is too deep. The lyrics say what your heart longs to believe, and the songs we sing are the faith you desperately need. The world pushes and pulls you and drags you around. Your heart is trampled and aches at the sound. The melody feels false and true as you are torn in two. You want to believe, and you want Him to come through. So sit and listen while I sing for you. This is our song, and some day you will sing too.

LIFE IS HARD. IT MIGHT sound obvious, but I don't just mean your life. I mean all life. Life is seriously hard-for everyone. Although we all grapple with hurt, insecurity, loss, and fear, we can become isolated and alone in our struggles. We need to hear each other's stories to remind us of our commonalities and to give us hope that we too can make it through the hard parts. God made life because there is so much more in it than the pain. In the struggles of living, there is brilliance and beauty: you.

There is a story worth telling in you. I don't know your story, but I will try to tell you the story of how I came to find a hallelujah in the brokenness of life in hopes that it will give you a voice to discover and sing your own broken hallelujah.

....

My life was a bowling ball released with impeccable form headed down the center of the lane. Sounds ideal, doesn't it? The truth is the weight in the ball and the inability to find traction on a lane waxed to perfection were leading me to a loud, messy collision.

A few years ago, I bought myself a new Bible. In the cover, I wrote the Bible was purchased with the hopes I could find the faith to believe God's love was for me. How does a girl who was raised in a preacher's home, educated at a Christian college, and married to a pastor get to the point she no longer believes God's love is for her?

I'd seen and experienced too much to deny God's existence and activity with our world, and I had studied too much to deny who he was. However, life, my life in particular, made it difficult to reconcile the God of my theology with the God of my faith. My faith was broken because I was broken.

....

Look, there in the back of the classroom, I'm the teacher watching a presentation on the use of the atomic bomb in WWII. I look pretty normal standing behind the desks observing the students, but look closer. Yes, you see them now, the tears: quiet, warm tears. They are softly pouring down my face; they just do that lately. If I am not fully occupied, they come. They push their way out of me, releasing the sorrow I refuse to share. Now that I've let you see this moment, you must be expecting me to explain the tears, but I cannot. The presentation is over, and I have work to do.

....

In my life, I have learned there is no ache like the ache of empty. Empty wombs, empty arms, empty beds, and empty chairs at the table: these are the empty spaces. These are longing and aching representations of the heart with pieces that have fallen out of place. What was I to do with empty? Yeah, you guessed it: try to fill it. Fill it until it is cramming and sore with the stretching and pulling of fullness. One more cookie, one more drink, one more kiss, one more project, one more mile: I needed more. I needed to fill that space. I was so full it hurt, but that spot refused to close. It just taunted me with its dissatisfied ache.

....

It is not far from Mother's Day, and I am not in my classroom today. Instead I am at a funeral for my mother's cousin who died in a motorcycle accident. A group of us are discussing the oddity of Jalit, my cousin, not coming since she lives only a stone's throw from the church. Maybe we should stop by her home because we haven't had the opportunity to meet baby Harley. We are tired, and it is a long drive home. Maybe another day.

....

Less than a week later I sat on a couch in my aunt's home in a state of shock and grief as an officer confirmed the causes of death for my cousin and her baby: Jalit had taken in more sugar than her body could process due to gestational diabetes, and without Jalit, Harley was alone. There was no one there to hold her, no one there to change her diaper, and no one there to feed her. My aunt wept in a ball on her floor crying out all the "if onlys": *if only she had realized something was wrong, if only she had stopped by or called, if only someone had heard the hungry cries of Harley....*

I told you- life is hard. It is really, really hard. Remember seeing me cry in the back of the classroom? Now you know some of it. Unfortunately, this is just one piece of the story leading up to a broken faith. Even now, tears sting my eyes and refuse to be confined. My heart breaks again and again when I crack the door to my past open to view what has been. There is more behind that door. Eventually I will show you, but I have to pace myself to stay intact.

At Jalit and Harley's funeral, two of Jalit's siblings led worship. One of the songs they sang was "How He Loves" by David Crowder Band. Over ten years earlier this same family had unexpectedly lost their father, my Uncle Nate, to head trauma that occurred while playing basketball. In the midst of pain and heartbreak that seems to be on replay in our family, they sang of God's love without any indication of doubt. They were singing:

If his grace is an ocean, we're all sinking.
And Heaven meets earth like an unforeseen kiss,
And my heart turns violently inside of my chest,
I don't have time to maintain these regrets,
When I think about the way...
He loves us,
Oh, how He loves us,

I didn't know how they could do it. Instead of feeling like I was sinking into God's grace, I felt like I was drowning in doubt and sorrow.

Five months earlier I'd experienced my first miscarriage, and I was still wrestling with the pain of a lost child as we stood in the same sanctuary as we had for a funeral only a week prior. We had come together, like so many times before, to mourn tragic and senseless loss. I stood there singing words I desperately wanted to be true. I wanted to believe that God loves us so.

After that funeral, every time I stood in a sanctuary singing "How He Loves," I would begin to feel the ache of empty inside. I could not sing without feeling overcome with sorrow and separation. My heart was torn. I deeply believed in God; I just couldn't believe in that kind of love from him, no matter how much I wanted it to be true. Then, ever so slowly, God changed something: me.

My story involves sexual abuse, the deaths of many family members, miscarriages, and a failing marriage. My faith was broken by the unspeakable acts of others, the difficulties of life, and the mistakes I made as I struggled to cope. However, over time, the prayer I had written in my Bible was answered, and I was able to believe God's love was for me. Now I sing "How He Loves" in worship instead of longing. Despite all the pain in my heart, I have been able to find a hallelujah because the empty ache has been filled with an understanding of God's love for me personally. It is my prayer that my story will open your story and that you, too, will find your hallelujah. I wrote this for you.

The Lord is close to the brokenhearted; he rescues those
whose spirits are crushed.
Psalm 34:18 (NLT)

Part 1

THE UNSPEAKABLE ACTS OF OTHERS

Man fails, but God's love doesn't

Chapter 1
MY FIRST WOUND

Wide eyed and innocent, the child is defiled
Safety, trust, and intimacy forever skewed.

In the dark, fear still creeps into the room,
But the beast is no longer under the bed.
The monster has moved to the head.

BAD DREAMS, STRANGE FEARS, HIDDEN memories with glimpses of reality, and a deep need to be perfect- these were some of the signs of the trauma from which my young mind had tried to shelter itself. I had experienced something as a child that was beyond my ability to understand, and in my innocence I had coped by pretending the confusion and pain did not exist. Unfortunately, that coping mechanism was built by a child, and it failed me as an adult when the world refused to stay in the order I demanded from it.

What happened to me, happens to so many children. It is something our developing minds and inexperienced emotions cannot process. It breaks something inside of us, and it is inexplicably difficult to understand the full impact of those moments. I struggle to come straight out and say what occurred: on one hand that is because I blocked out the moments of the experience itself, and on the other it is because a deed done to the innocent is unspeakable. The monster under my bed was a man my family and I trusted. He sexually molested me, and I was forever marked by his deeds.

As a teenager, I received a letter of apology from this man for what he had done. I had no idea what to do with that. It opened a wound I had been trying to deny existed. Not for the last time, I began to wonder where God was when I needed him. I was angry- really angry- that he didn't stop my molester. I knew God had the power to stop him and to stop the effects of his actions. Wasn't God's presence supposed to mean protection from pain? It wasn't until many years later that I learned God's presence means standing beside me in the middle of the moment my heart is being broken.

During my journey to restore my faith in God's great love for me personally, my husband and I were reading *The Magician's Nephew* by C.S. Lewis with our children. One night, I found myself crying as I read a passage to my young, eager audience. In the passage, Digory asks Aslan to heal his sick mother. Aslan tells Digory that he cannot do it in that moment because there is a bigger plan:

"But please, please -won't you- can't you give me something that will cure Mother?"

Up till then he had been looking at the Lion's great feet and the huge claws on them; now, in his despair, he looked up at its face. What he saw surprised him as much as anything in his whole life. For the tawny face was bent down near his own and (wonder of wonders) great shining tears stood in the Lion's eyes. They were such big, bright tears compared with Digory's own that for a moment he felt as if the Lion must really be sorrier about his Mother than he was himself.

"My son, my son," said Aslan. "I know. Grief is great."

The words jumped from the page to my heart. It was the tears. They had me. I have understood there is a bigger picture for quite some time. However, there was something added to my understanding this time: tears. It was not my picture of a cold and calculating God standing idle as a world spins around me. Instead, I could see our God with big fat tears and pain in his eyes for me. I saw a God who understands my grief and is moved with compassion for me. In that moment, a piece of my heart was made full.

The most mind boggling thing about God is the fact that he is big enough to hold the entire world in his hands but also willing to be small enough to make himself available to me. This is hard to comprehend. However, many of the problems we face in this life come because he loves me the same as he loves everyone else in the world. In order for that love to take its fullest form, he has to allow us to make choices. Sometimes choices made by others crush us, and sometimes our choices crush others. Although the choices made by each of us can cause great damage, God is not limited in his ability to use every part of our lives.

Almost everyone has been hurt by someone. The greatest hurts seem to come from those whom we have trusted to care for us. For some, divorce has left them questioning what a promise really means. Others have been betrayed by friends or family. There is physical, sexual, and emotional abuse in so many of our stories. Whatever the exact scenario is, damage has been done, and it can feel like no one can be trusted, including God. We look at all the hurt, and we wonder why God would allow it in our lives. Although he permits those he loves the freedom to do actions that can cause damage, he stands beside those who are being broken. He is there as our worlds crumble and what seems like chaos ensues.

While we are close to the damaging moments, we don't get to see how the hurtful actions of others can be part of a beautiful story. It is especially hard to see how God could possibly be demonstrating his unfailing love in those moments. It can be easier to see this when viewing someone else's life. The story of Joseph gives us an opportunity to see a story of God's presence within the moments of brokenness. It also demonstrates God's ability to redeem the unspeakable acts of others.

If anyone understood the hurt caused by those close to him, it was Joseph. The story of Joseph reminds us that God is present when the betrayals of others put us in pits and prisons. It can be a challenge to stare at the walls of those pits and prisons of life and imagine that we, like Joseph, could someday live in the palace. There are two facts in Joseph's story we can apply to our stories: God has an unfailing, passionate, and pursuing love for us, and he has a plan to bring the dreams he has given us to completion no matter what circumstances we find ourselves in. He is there in the midst of the broken mess, and he desires for us to receive his love and the plans he has for us.

God gave Joseph dreams of leadership. Soon after Joseph received these dreams, his life took a course that made those dreams seem like an impossibility. His brothers had jealous hearts, so they plotted to kill him. Eventually, they decided to sell him into slavery instead. Although Joseph may have benefited from a little more humility, he did not end up in slavery by his own actions or choices. Like so many of us, Joseph was betrayed by those closest to him.

While in slavery, Joseph was blessed. God did not remove him from the difficult circumstances; he blessed Joseph in the midst of them. He was raised to a position of responsibility, but he was still a slave. For a time, I was angry with God because I could only see how I had been wounded. I thought God should have prevented the circumstances, and that is where I focused. I struggled to see the blessings in the middle of the hurt. Joseph, too, could have focused on the hurt and betrayal his brothers caused, but he recognized the blessing God had given him. He demonstrated this when he was given the opportunity to have Potipher's wife. Scripture indicates he refused her because he valued the blessing of God in his life.

Despite his faithfulness, Joseph's situation became worse. He went from being a slave to being a prisoner. Potipher's wife lied about him, and he paid the price. Once again, the acts of others did damage to Joseph. Some of you might find this easy to relate to because it is your story. You are faithfully serving God, but you go from one damaging relationship to another. You are trusting God and striving to succeed in the midst of the pain caused by others, and just when you are finding some stability, someone close pulls the rug out from under you.

When you are experiencing great strife at the hands of others, it can be difficult to see God's unfailing, passionate, and pursuing love for you. Joseph's story helps us to remember God's love is still a part of our stories. Genesis 39:2, 21, and 23 tell us that God was with Joseph, giving him success in everything he did, and (pay close attention here) it says God demonstrated his faithful love. During this chapter, Joseph had gone from being a slave to being a prisoner, yet the text says God was showing Joseph his faithful love. I'm not sure whether Joseph could recognize this faithful love in those moments or not. I know I would have really struggled to see a transition from a slave to a prisoner as a demonstration of unfailing love. Yet, there is no denying the text states that God was showing Joseph unfailing love, which is easier to understand when we get to the end of Joseph's story. Unfortunately, we don't get to jump ahead to the endings of our stories to see how God's unfailing love is being demonstrated in our messy moments of life.

Sometimes we view the circumstances of our lives as prisons. We feel as though our situations continually go from bad to worse, trapping us and causing us to wonder how God could possibly be showing us unfailing love. The truth is unchanged by your perspective on your circumstances; you are loved right this moment, in the middle of your situation, with an unfailing love. God is absolutely with you, and he is passionate about you. Although your circumstances may cause you to feel as though you are abandoned, Joseph's God of unfailing love is the same God of unfailing love today. You might be in the center of some terrible situations beyond your control, but you do not know the end of your story. You do not know all of how God is using what the world meant to harm you for his good.

Although his situation must have felt as though it had gone from bad to worse, God used Joseph's time in prison to help others understand the dreams God had given them and to further his plan for Joseph's life. Even after Joseph interpreted the dreams, he was forgotten by man. He was left in prison for two more years. Here Joseph sat, abandoned and used by man. If we didn't know the end of the story, it would be easy to say God had forgotten Joseph and the dreams of leadership he had been given.

You might be wondering what happened to the dreams God put on your heart. The world is knocking you down again and again, and you are wondering if God really is present. *Oh, he exists, but is he really with me? He loves the world, but does he love me?* The answer to these questions is a resounding, "YES!" Again, I know this is true because the God of yesterday is the God of today. The Bible reveals his nature to us, and Joseph's life is just one example of God's activity in the lives of humanity. It gives us a chance to see a bigger story while we feel trapped in the moments of our own stories.

Joseph had to be in the prison in order to be in the palace. He had to be forgotten and abandoned by the cup bearer he had helped so he could be remembered when it mattered. It may feel as though you are forgotten by God as those around you leave their marks, but he is right beside you with an unfailing love. He is preparing you for the rest of the story.

Joseph's circumstances had no indication of improving. Yet, when asked to interpret the Pharaoh's dreams, Joseph says, "It is beyond my power to do this, but God can tell you what it means and set you at ease." (Genesis 41:16 NLT) Joseph must have had a deep understanding of God's unfailing love because he still believed God given dreams were meant to bring us peace in our hearts. Peace comes from knowing God is active and involved. A few verses later, Joseph tells Pharaoh

God would do what was given in the dreams. Despite the fact that he had been greatly abused and neglected by those closest to him and was yet to see his own dreams come true, Joseph believed God fulfills the dreams he gives to us.

Oh, if only I had lived my life like Joseph! If only I had not let the pain of life pile up so high I could not see past it. However, God knows the bigger picture. He knows the full story, and he can use our failures to make something beautiful, just like he used the failures of Joseph's family.

In Genesis 45: 5-8 and Genesis 50:19,20 Joseph tells his brothers God had a plan all along. The terrible circumstances Joseph found himself in were the circumstances necessary to bring Joseph to a place in which he could not only see his dreams fulfilled but be used to save the lives of his family and many, many others. In this story, we see God's unfailing love is not just demonstrated to Joseph, but it is also made evident to his brothers, the very people who hurt Joseph.

Although Joseph's brothers acted in a wicked and deceitful manner, God demonstrated his love for them by bringing Joseph to a position to preserve their lives in the famine. God was faithful in his love and in his plan for the lives of the children of Jacob (Israel). Admittedly, I feel slightly indignant God would demonstrate the same love he shows me to the man who molested me and many others. At the same time, I am overwhelmed with gratitude for a love this big. What kind of love is willing to demonstrate grace and mercy to those of us who do great damage to others? This is the love God has for each and every one of us.

In my own story, I struggled to see God's love in the midst of circumstances that did not line up with the dreams I believed he had given me. Because of the pain in my life, I felt God had forgotten me and my dreams. On the other side of a lot of counseling sessions, prayer, and study, I see how God had not forgotten me or watched in cold disconnect as I struggled. One of the dreams God put on my heart at a young age was to write, and little did I know, I needed to live in the pits and prisons in order for the dream to come to fruition. God knew the message I was to write, and I could not get there without God allowing me to experience both the brokenness of life and his ability to make it into something beautiful. He stayed close beside me with a heavy heart as the world did its worst. He felt the hurt with me, but he also knew what was to come. He knew what he could do with the mess and the damage of my life. He loved me enough, he loved my molester enough, and he loved you enough to allow the world to crash around me.

Scripture is full of examples of God's faithful love to mankind. It is God's nature to love you. Hold on to your God given dreams. You are not forgotten; you are loved with an unfailing, passionate and pursuing love. God knows your circumstances, and he is with you in this moment. He is walking with you, and he is using your circumstances to fulfill his purposes. Hold tight to the knowledge of his love and his faithfulness.

We can rejoice, too, when we run into problems and trials, for we know that they help us develop endurance. and endurance develops strength of character, and character strengthens our confident hope of salvation. and this hope will not lead to disappointment. For we know how dearly God loves us, because he has given us the Holy Spirit to fill our hearts with his love.
Romans 5:3-5 (NLT)

<u>Your Voice</u>

Take some time to reflect on your own story.

If you are studying this as a group, please allow people room to keep their stories private if they so choose. Each person should only share as he or she feels comfortable. However, don't rush through the questions as some individuals may need more time to think and process their own stories.

As you share, be sure to be clear about what you would like to be kept among the group and what is okay for others to repeat.

1. Are there wounds in your life that have been caused by those close to you? If so, how has this impacted your view of God?

2. What are some of the ways God has blessed you? Have any of those occurred while you were experiencing a time of heartache and pain?

3. What are some of the dreams God has put on your heart? Tell about how you have seen God use painful circumstances to fulfill those dreams, or how the broken moments you are in now might be bringing you closer to fulfilling those dreams.

If you cannot see God using the hurtful moments to fulfill your God given dreams, write a prayer in the area provided for question three. Thank God for blessings you have and ask him to reveal his love and give you hope for the future.

Chapter 2

EMMA'S BROKEN HALLELUJAH

Daddy's love was strong and sour.
Spirit scented breath warned her to disappear,
But his words and his fists found their marks.
She ran to the arms of rescue
Only to find his love to be strong and sour.

THIS IS EMMA'S STORY:

My father was a high functioning alcoholic with a good job. Holidays were always full of him going around the house wrecking everything, throwing things across the room and screaming and yelling. If I wanted to talk to my dad about something I had to catch him after the first beer and before the third. Life growing up was a constant uncertainty. Never knowing if it would be a nice family evening or a night of screaming and fire in the pit of your stomach.

I grew up thinking that was normal-that was what every man was like. That is the background for my marriage. I went from living with one alcoholic to another. In a lot of ways, this lead me to believe my husband's behaviors were totally normal. I lived in a middle class "Christian" family, but I'd never had a Godly man in my life. Because my husband went to church every Sunday, I thought I had a good one. Don't get me wrong, my husband is an amazing man... when he is sober.

We truly love each other with a God given love. However, he is a totally different person when he is drunk. He becomes verbally and, occasionally, physically abusive. He never has the intention to hurt anyone. It is a twelve pack in two hours kind of thing. When he is drunk, he has no idea what he is like, and he doesn't believe what I tell him about it when he is sober. You never think a life like this will be yours when you are a Christian girl marrying a Christian man.

I'm not outgoing, and I am extremely loyal to the few people I let close to me. This accentuates the pain my husband causes. The pain is so deep because the one I love, the one I have really let into my heart, causes my hurt over and over. At one point, the pain felt like I was going to die even if it wasn't physically. It brought out my own refining fire. I tried everything to be the good Christian wife. He'd knock me down, and I'd get up and forgive. I was being trampled to the ground for doing my best to love him. How do you survive when the person you love so much and who is supposed to cherish you, love you, and protect you is doing all they can to grind you into the ground, and they don't even remember doing it?

Abuse and alcoholism are something we don't talk about. My extended family told me not to tell anyone about my husband's behaviors. My husband has business associates at church, so even there I have not been able to talk about my struggles because of the possible social and business ramifications. I have been going to counseling on and off, and I have finally shared with a few people recently.

With the exception of one woman from church, the people I talked to said to leave my husband. She was in the midst of her own trials, and she told me to stay. My heart was not at peace with leaving, and she was the only one to say it would be okay to stay. I don't remember the details of her spiritual advice, just that she said over and over to stay unless I am in severe physical danger- don't leave; stick it out.

We reached a point- because I began to fear for the physical safety of my family- where I made it clear to my husband that he could have his family or his alcohol. He is fighting now for his family. He attends AA and meets with a pastor. He still struggles, but the drunken abusive behaviors are occurring less often. It was a seven day a week occurrence. Now it is more like three weeks out of three months.

I can't change him. I can only rely on God. God is changing me. I can make poor choices, or I can cling to God. This has been a struggle in my own life. I decided for years that God never even heard my prayers, so why bother. I still visit that place occasionally.

Although I'm still in the midst of it, I'm sharing because God hasn't given up on our marriage or me and my dreams. God can still use me. I wish I had known other women's stories when I was in the worst of it. I want others to know that if I can make it through this, you can make it through your situation.

Emma's Voice

1. Are there wounds in your life that have been caused by those close to you? If so, how has this impacted your view of God?

Yes! I have been verbally and physically abused by both my father and my husband, which means I've been abused nearly my entire life. At first I believed like a child, but as the wounds became deeper and I became older, I decided God was distant, uncaring, and did not hear me. I thought, *why bother with him*? I still believed and wanted to be saved, but I unconsciously kept him at arm's length. I felt a God who allowed so much pain and oppression obviously did not care about me on a personal level. As the wounds became worse and worse, I knew I was going to die if I didn't find him. That's when I sought him with all my heart and learned what it means to have a relationship with him. If it had not been for my trials and pain, I would still be a lukewarm Christian today.

2. What are some of the ways God has blessed you? Have any of those occurred while you were experiencing a time of heartache and pain?

It is hard to see the blessings in the midst of the worst moments. Some have been tangible, amazing gifts that I know came from God. More important though, God has provided me with an amazing church and friends who accepted me as the wreck I was – and still am! It was also in that dark endless tunnel, abandoned and so deeply hurt by those supposed to love and protect me that I found him: *Jesus*. In writing this, it's not rehashing the hurt and the pain that brings tears to my eyes, but it's *Jesus*. I now question the state of my salvation before all the pain and the suffocating darkness that brought me to seek him. I don't need to see the demons to know when I am surrounded, but now I know that I know that I know the power and love of Christ. I have experienced that power that makes demons flee and the joy that makes me dance in the midst of despair. I spent so much time in tears crying out to God, and he came and sat beside me. The pain and trials aren't over, but I'm not alone, and I know he will give me what I need to make it through each day.

3. **What are some of the dreams that God has put on your heart? Tell about how you have seen God use painful circumstances to fulfill those dreams, or how the broken moments you are in now might be bringing you closer to fulfilling those dreams.**

Once upon a time I was going to change the world. There is no other way to describe my dreams but BIG. I was on fire! God gifted me academically and physically to achieve nearly anything. But after getting married I became a prisoner to the secrets and the complete wreck of my life. I was unable to finish college and had a dead end job I hated (a job which, I found out, was really only paying for my husband's addictions). I've watched the years slip away and the dreams sat in a pool of bitterness in my heart before I *finally* realized I lacked both the wisdom and the discipline needed to achieve them. The burning desire has now been replaced with a quiet watchfulness. I still sometimes get consumed with the what ifs, but I know that God will do something with my dreams one day, as long as I keep my eyes on him and follow his will.

Chapter 3

GOD'S LOVE IS UNFAILING

THE DAMAGES CAUSED BY OTHERS can cause us to doubt God's love for us. However, scripture demonstrates repeatedly that God is not like man, and his love will never fail us. I have seen the words "unfailing love" jump off the screen of my phone again and again this past year as I have been completing a Bible in a year reading plan. It has amazed me how many times the words appear. As soon as I started to look for them, the more I was aware of their presence. I finally quit highlighting the verses because there were just so many.

Generally, in literature, when something is repeated, it is because it is something important the author really wants to be sure the reader understands. Although there were many human authors involved, God, the divine author, remained consistent in his message to mankind. The presentation of his love as an "unfailing love" is no exception. I didn't notice these words as I had read in the past because I didn't need them or understand their importance as much as I have in the last few years.

It is amazing how rich and full the scriptures are. God is so big and so complex, and his love for us is so deep. When we read our Bibles we cannot get it all in one reading. I have read my Bible throughout my entire life, and I am still struck by new understandings, new confirmations, new convictions, and new healing in my own life as the Spirit leads me to receive what God knows I need for that season of my life. I encourage you to keep reading. God's word is his love letter to us. He reveals who he is because he desires to be known by us. He is ever drawing us closer to him. He is ever pursuing our hearts.

We live in a culture of convenient love relationships. People are told again and again to follow their hearts. The problem with this advice is the heart of man is fickle and easily deceived. It seems to be human nature to fail one another as our hearts' desires change with the tides. Thankfully, God's nature is unchanging. Throughout scripture, God demonstrates his ability to love his people despite their constant turning from him and his desire for us to allow him to help us love others the way he loves us. He wants us to know his love, and he desires to fill our hearts with love for others.

In some ways, the concept of an unfailing love can be difficult for us to understand. We do not see this type of love demonstrated on a day to day basis when we look at the behaviors of others. It is rare to see people choose to love another person when the going gets tough. In fact, sometimes we look at people's actions and agree that they are not deserving of an unswerving love. It is often easier for us to understand broken relationships than relationships that never give up. This might be part of the reason scripture has to repeat the same message to us again and again: God loves us, no matter what we do and no matter what is done to us. He is unchanging, and his love is unfailing.

Malachi 3:6 says, "I am the LORD, and I do not change. That is why you descendants of Jacob are not already destroyed. Ever since the days of your ancestors, you have scorned my decrees and failed to obey them" (NLT). God does not quit loving, even when he has good reason to. Every scripture that teaches us of the nature of God's unfailing love rings as true today as it ever did. God does not change. His love does not fail.

I have chosen a few of the verses about God's unfailing love in order to give a general sense of what scripture states repeatedly about one aspect of God's love. The first verse is from Jonah because it demonstrates some of the feelings I have held onto from time to time in relationship to God's love for those, like the man who molested me, who have caused great pain. I haven't always agreed with God's decision to love all people, except I know I need a love this great to extend to me also.

Jonah didn't want to warn Nineveh of God's wrath because he knew God's nature was to love people despite their failings. Jonah 4:2 says, "So he complained to the LORD about it: 'Didn't I say before I left home that you would do this, LORD? That is why I ran away to Tarshish! I knew that you are a merciful God, slow to get angry and filled with unfailing love. You are eager to turn back from destroying people" (NLT). Jonah had tried to run from the message God sent him to give because he knew God would just forgive Nineveh instead of destroy them. He knew that he knew that he knew that God is full of unfailing love. He didn't like it, but he knew it. He wanted his prediction of what would happen to Nineveh to come to pass. He didn't want God to extend grace and mercy to the people of Nineveh.

Don't be too quick to judge Jonah because there might just be a few people in the world you wouldn't mind if God would choose to destroy instead of love unfailingly. In the manner God loved Joseph and his brothers with the same unfailing love, he loves you and those who cause you great pain with the same unfailing love. It isn't easy to reconcile, but it is a truth you may find yourself grateful for if you are the one causing the pain in someone else's life.

The Psalms are jam packed with songs and prayers that declare and call upon God's unfailing love. In Psalm 145:14-15 the psalmist says, "The LORD helps the fallen and lifts those bent beneath their loads. The eyes of all look to you in hope; you give them their food as they need it" (NLT). God does not abandon those in need. He provides all we need. This is why one could come before God in confidence and say: "The LORD will work out his plans for my life-- for your faithful love, O LORD, endures forever. Don't abandon me, for you made me" (Psalm 138:8 NLT). Just as God worked out his plans in Joseph's life, he will work his plans out in your life. Man may fail, but God never will.

In a string of statements repeating "His faithful love endures forever", Psalm 136:23 states, "He remembered us in our weakness. His faithful love endures forever" (NLT). Weak, strong, sick, healthy, wicked, righteous, it doesn't matter your state: God's love for you is unfailing. There is scripture after scripture highlighting this simple truth.

I will close with this passage from Micah 7:19-20: "Once again you will have compassion on us. You will trample our sins under your feet and throw them into the depths of the ocean! You will show us your faithfulness and unfailing love as you promised to our ancestors Abraham and Jacob long ago" (NLT). God's promise to Abraham and Jacob is our promise today. We are joint heirs with the father, and we are adopted through Christ into the family of God. We can live confident, no matter what may be thrown our way by a broken people, God's love for us is unfailing.

PART 2

THE BROKENNESS
OF LIVING

You can lose everything else in life, but God's love will remain present.

Chapter 4

THE BREAKING
THAT FOLLOWED

I remember.

I remember lying on my back in the middle of sit ups and breathing in a deep sense of loss and confusion at the news I had just heard. Life, energy, and vitality were interrupted when Uncle Nate's life ended abruptly.

I remember coming back early to the hollow, empty dorms of Christmas break. Here I received the news of my grandmother's passing, and here I stood with tears and water streaming down my body in a long shower of grief.

I remember Aunt Judy's home cramped with a hospital bed, our bodies, and a heavy sadness in the singing of a hymn. I longed for her enduring smile and joy to fill the room again.

I remember the hard pews of a small church where we gathered to honor Angie's life. Her sons were later my students, and I sat around a conference table aching while other teachers, unaware of my connection, discussed the tragedy.

I remember stepping into a crowded hospital elevator with my friends after a visit with Aunt Kathy. My conflicted prayers asking for someone else's life to end so she could live stopped when her heart could take no more.

I remember the buzz of my students in the cafeteria as I prayed desperately for my infant nephew, Nathaniel, to live. I can still see the world slipping by the window of my car as I wept on the way to his funeral.

I remember, and I remember, and I remember....

I THOUGHT I WOULD START this book with the line, "Who hasn't sung 'It is Well with My Soul' at a funeral?", but then I realized probably a lot of people had never experienced this event that had become fairly common in mine. Not everyone experiences a stretch of fourteen years in which they almost average a funeral per year.

I have sung "It is Well with My Soul" and really felt at peace, and I've also sung the same song with bitter tears streaming down my face because it most definitely was not well with my soul. Honestly, I have sung that song in hurt and anger toward a God who had allowed events that led to me standing at yet another funeral singing the same heart wrenching song. I was tired of the part of my life that lined up with "when sorrows like sea billows roll." I wanted the "peace like a river." Many times, I sang with pain in my heart at the loss of the person we mourned that day combined with the pain of recollecting all the others.

Because doubt had crept into my heart and mind, many church worship services highlighted the battle within me. I cannot begin to tell you the number of times I have stood and sang hymns and choruses in which my heart ached because I was completely torn up inside. I was desperately wanting the God to whom I was singing to hear me. I wanted answers, and I wanted to feel for once, just this once, when it really counted, he would show up. I sang with the pain of one whose faith was in turmoil. Why were my prayers unanswered? Where was God's love in the loss? How can I have faith to believe he is holding me when it feels my world is slipping away one life at a time?

I am part of a large, close family. Although my father was an only child, my mother was one of eight children. Large families have many big events: reunions, weddings, babies, and burials. This is why, for a long season, death seemed to be stuck on repeat. Funerals were a regular part of the routine: Uncle Nate, Aunt Judy, Angie, Grandma Richardson, Aunt Kathy, Donny, Uncle Bill, Grandma Hampton, Nathaniel, Terry, Jalit, Harley, Karina Rose (my first miscarriage) and Judah Thomas or Ava Grace (my second miscarriage). Many of the people on this list were young- quite young. Some were simply family, and some were family I loved deeply. The loss of each one left another space in my wounded heart.

....

Donny stood in the doorway of the apartment my husband and I shared after a day of packing. As we were saying our goodbyes, he told me how much the time we had shared in Springfield, MO had meant to him. Growing up, he had always wanted to live closer to his cousins, so the weekend card games, meals, and general hang out time over the past year had been very meaningful to him.

A couple years later, I stood outside a hotel room door in Florida gripping a cell phone while my mother delivered the news there would be no more card games, no more meals, and no more time together. The time for saying goodbye had come and gone.

At the age of twenty-four, Donny's heart stopped working. Donny was my family, and he was my friend. His funeral was held in a small church in central New York. We buried him in the same graveyard we had buried many others, including his mother. When he died, another empty crevice formed within me.

....

I don't think I have ever fully grieved some of the losses. I've told myself I don't have the same right to the grief as others. It wasn't my parent or my sibling. Yet with each funeral the grief of the other losses came to mingle with the grief of the moment. With every death I felt a new ache, a new empty.

The world was slipping, and I was grasping to control it. I wanted to tame it and make it stay in order. I was tired of losing. I was tired of hurting. I didn't see God in the loss. I saw pain, more pain, and sorrow. I wanted it to stop... but it wouldn't. It just kept coming...wave after wave.

I wasn't the type to open up about the hurt. I just kept living. I kept the dishes done and the counters clean. I ran; I worked; I played with and cared for my children; I did life, but I did it with great care to never release the emotions bubbling beneath the surface. I was determined to keep a firm grasp on life. I wasn't going to let any hurt creep out. I had a sense that if I let myself go a little, I might not be able to come back. The sorrows of my heart mixed together with the shame of my childhood experience. I needed control. I had to be perfect. I had to prove I was worth it. I was somebody. Every flaw was a glaring mark I could not tolerate. It chipped away at the sanity I was grasping.

Those who have known me over the years would likely be surprised by this since I appeared to have almost everything together. It was easier to be busy. It was easier to live exactly in the moment or look to the future... never back. What good was behind me? Plenty of it, but mixed in was the loss of the good. It was the people I loved slipping away. No more card games, no more sitting in the sunroom laughing, no more hot rolls with butter. It was tombstones marking the end. No, I didn't want to stop and think about that. I wanted to be in the moment, and I wanted to make sure I was safe from the emotion. Emotion was vulnerability, and vulnerability was weakness, and weakness leads to abuse. Yeah, I was messed up. I was broken.

How did this mix with God's love? How could I trust Him and be open to him? This is where the conflict hit. I believed in God. I believed deeply in him. I couldn't deny my experiences with him. I could not deny his deity. I could not deny his presence in my life. Yet, each death chipped away at my ability to open myself to receive his love. Spirituality is a combination of the head and the heart. I was off balance because my head knew more than my heart could open up to receive. My heart was telling me my head had to be wrong.

Job understood feeling abandoned by God rather than doubting his existence. Job lost everything, and there was no one to point his finger at but God. Job did not deny God was real, instead he questioned why God had turned his back on him. In Job 30:20-22 Jobs says, "I cry to you, O God, but you don't answer. I stand before you, but you don't even look. You have become cruel toward me. You use your power to persecute me. You throw me into the whirlwind and destroy me in the storm" (NLT). Job had lost his entire family, his fortune, and his health. He was hurt, and he was angry. He wanted God to give him answers. He could not see how what he was experiencing lined up with his theology.

I too wanted answers from God. I wanted to know why he would destroy the faithful. I wanted to know why he had removed his loving hands from my family, which served him completely. I wanted my answers because I was tired of singing songs on Sunday mornings that felt empty to me week after week. I wanted to sing about God's love in appreciation for a love that I could feel. I wanted to sing the line, "Oh how he loves," and believe it with every fiber of my being, but I could not.

How do we explain a God who allows pain that was not caused by other's free will? How do we explain the illnesses, the empty wombs, and the freak accidents that steal joy and life? For some, the question is formed in the depths of a depression that appeared without obvious cause. The question of God's love is often born in the lack of explanation.

Like Job, we really want answers. Job had lived an upright life, and he wanted to know why he was suffering. His friends gave him many answers, but none were satisfactory, especially since most of those answers included accusations against Job's character. Job wanted justification. He wanted a chance to plead his case with God. He felt his suffering was undeserved, and he wanted to hear from God why his upright life was receiving punishment. He didn't get the answer he was expecting. Instead, he received a glimpse of who God is, and in that glimpse he received more than any explanation could provide.

God pointed Job to the majesty of creation. He highlighted the immense and the detailed awe inspiring work of his hands. It is Job who is called to answer when God says, "Do you still want to argue with the Almighty? You are God's critic, but do you have the answers?" (Job 40:2 NLT). God's answer to Job points out mankind cannot truly fathom all of who God is or all the plans he has for creation. Our minds cannot see the full picture, we can only see the pieces closest to us. Rather than receiving an answer of explanation, Job got an answer of why the explanation is too complex for the human mind to comprehend.

As frustrating as this may sound at first, there is deep beauty in it. Who wants to serve a God so small that we can explain and understand all he is? If God is not greater than we can fathom, why should we worship and serve him? There is a peace in understanding God's control of the world is bigger than we can comprehend.

What changed everything for Job was not an explanation of his personal circumstances, it was an encounter with God. In Job chapter 42:2-6, Job speaks about the alteration of his heart:

> "You asked, 'Who is this that questions my wisdom with such ignorance?' It is I- and I was talking about things I knew nothing about, things far too wonderful for me. You said, 'Listen and I will speak! I have some questions for you, and you must answer them.' I had only heard about you before, but now I have seen you with my own eyes. I take back everything I said, and I sit in dust and ashes to show my repentance." (NLT)

We look at God's answer to Job, and we realize we did not hang the stars in the sky. We were not there when God laid the foundation of the earth, and we do not know all he is or all he has planned. We simply have to know he is there, not just in the general sense- He is present in *our* circumstances. He understands our hurts and our pain, and he loves us. He loves us so very deeply that he was willing to show up as a man. He was willing to experience all the pain and sorrow of living so we could experience a relationship with him in a personal way. The God of the universe, the God of it all, the God beyond explanation, loves you-now there is a great mystery.

One of my favorite sermon illustrations was when my giant man of a husband talked about the distance of a small child looking up at a parent and how that changes when the parent comes down to the child's level. My six foot, two hundred sixty pound, football built husband made it real as he laid himself down on the dusty stage to demonstrate the way he allows our three children to come close and climb all over him. He was creating an image of how God laid himself on the floor of this earth to be close to his children, and he has not for a moment been excluded from the dirt and the grime of living. He is so big, and he makes himself so small so we can meet with him. He looks us in the eyes and says, "Be still and know that I am God" (Psalm 46:10).

It took God working on my heart in a variety of ways for me to begin to understand God knows the hurt and the depths of your despair. He has not turned his back on you. He is in control, regardless of your ability to understand. Your circumstances are not a removal of his hand from your life. If you listen, he will answer you. The answer is not an explanation of your piece of the picture, the answer is *you are part of the picture.* You are just a speck in the context of it all, yet he loves you. He is present in the mess and the ache. He is present in the death, the loss, the illness, and the depression. He is present in your situation. You are not abandoned or alone. You are loved by the one who is bigger than it all. His love for you is present.

<u>Your Voice</u>

Take some time to reflect on your own story.

If you are studying this as a group, please allow people room to keep their stories private if they so choose. Each person should only share as he or she feels comfortable. However, don't rush through the questions as some individuals may need more time to think and process their own stories.

As you share, be sure to be clear about what you would like to be kept among the group and what is okay for others to repeat.

1. Have there been painful experiences in your life that are simply the result of being alive (not caused by the actions of others or by your own actions)? If so, has this impacted your view of God?

2. What are the things in life that reveal God's active presence in the world? (The intricacy of creation, the birth of a child, a miraculous work… be specific about the things that speak to you individually.)

3. Does reflecting on God's active presence impact your perspective concerning God and the pain you have experienced? Do you see him in your situation, or do you see him as a distant observer?

If you cannot see God's presence in your life, write a prayer in the area provided for question three. Acknowledge his majesty beyond our understanding, and ask him to reveal his love for you personally in the middle of the expanse of the world.

Chapter 5

BROOKE'S BROKEN HALLELUJAH

I have been to death's door with my children. Three times Peter denied you, and I have not. Three days passed as you defeated the grave, yet three births were a battle. One baby could not stay to fight; while the others have escaped to sleep another night. My prayers, a war song I could not sing, left me silent and trembling.

THIS IS BROOKE'S STORY:

I grew up in a Christian home. I was always taught to not question God, that we didn't get angry because God was in control. I don't know if my parents ever outright told us not to be angry, but it was implied. It was easy to remain joyful because my home life was wonderful. I grew up in Africa, and my mom was always filled with joy. It was a rare occasion that she wasn't in a good mood. That joy was passed along to me, and I, generally, have lived content, secure, and happy.

As an adult, I began to experience some less wonderful parts of life. While my husband was in medical school and I was a Neonatal nurse, we tried for a year to get pregnant with our first child. The news we were finally pregnant with a baby boy put us over the moon. Early on, some of the joy was diminished as we found out he had a twin located in my fallopian tube that had to be removed. I was caught off guard by the grief I felt for the son I would not know.

The surviving baby, Austin, was born sixteen and a half weeks early. It shocked us both. I thought he was going to die, so I told my husband we just needed to enjoy him as long as we had him. We were heartbroken. I'll never forget when a friend prayed for us a day after Austin was born. Our friend said, "God, we are angry. We don't understand why this happened."

I never once opened my Bible during his three month NICU stay. I don't know why, but I just couldn't. I prayed a lot, and I felt the prayers of others. I felt lifted up by their prayers, just as Moses's hands were lifted up by Aaron and Hur during a battle. When Moses's hands were up, they were winning, and when they fell, they were losing. Without the supporting prayers of others, I might have lost hope. Austin came home from the NICU twelve weeks to the day he was born. He had no residual effects of being born at twenty-four weeks. I felt like we had experienced a modern day miracle. Babies just don't have stays as easy as his. He was my miracle.

With our first and second pregnancies, we had struggled with infertility for several years (including the use of IVF). This is why, after our second child, we were surprised to find out we had become pregnant again- and with twins! At thirty-one weeks, as expected, our twin girls,

Katie and Emma, were born early. Two days later, we found out Katie had a heart defect. She had a hole between her ventricles and her atria. She would need open heart surgery between the ages of two and six months of life. Our hearts sank. Our infant needed open heart surgery on bypass; they would stop and restart her heart.

We felt we'd been through enough. We started to question. *Why, God, did you allow us to go through the uncertainty of a twenty-four weeker and not one but two thirty-one weekers, only to add a heart defect in there?! Why? Why us; haven't we gone through enough? Did we not pray enough, trust enough?*

I felt like I had a broken baby. Heart babies were always the hard ones to take care of in the NICU. They are perfect on the outside, but all broken on the inside. Truth be told, we are all like that in many ways. We try to present a picture of perfection, but on the inside, we are messed up. We are broken.

Katie came home after eight weeks in the NICU. We were racing the clock: how big could we grow her to give her the best shot in surgery before she was in heart failure? I spent hours trying to feed this baby. She didn't want to eat. She spent all her energy just trying to be alive. They wanted her to be at least ten pounds for surgery.

Finally, at the end of the summer, our cardiologist said it was time because she wanted it done before flu and cold season. Katie was just about at ten pounds so we set the date, September fifteenth. I was in agony the month before her scheduled date. I cried, and I wept. As we came closer to surgery, I felt like I was losing my mind.

I sobbed and sobbed one night, feeling the weight of the devil heavily. I felt attacked. A true spiritual battle was going on. I was filled with fear; I had lost my joy. I called my mom, and she called my grandfather. They both prayed with me. I emailed some ladies from my Bible study and asked if they could come the next day. I needed them to hold me up in prayer-just like Moses needed his hands held up. I knew God could, once again, perform a miracle to bring my baby through to full health. But a doubt crept into my mind. *What if he didn't? How would I get through that? What would I tell my kids? What would I say when they asked why God let that happen?* And I struggled.

A best friend drove down to be with me during Katie's surgery. This meant the world to me, and it reassured me God was looking out for me. The love and support of others reminded me of God's presence in the situation. Katie made it through surgery, and she came home in record time. I was grateful God had brought Katie through, but something in me began to doubt he would provide for the health and safety of my family.

These experiences made a crack in my faith. The fear and doubt had left place for Satan to creep in and plant more seeds of fear and doubt. I struggled for weeks. I was fearful to even leave the house. I cried in the shower asking God why I felt so lost. Why didn't I feel like myself? Why was I so fearful? I lived fearful something was going to happen to me, my kids, or my husband. I spent a lot of time praying and pleading with God. I wanted to feel like me again- my normal, happy, joyful self.

I spent time in scripture, but I only told my husband about my struggle. Although I had shared when the battle was for my children, I didn't have any Christian friends I felt like sharing this with. I went off social media because I couldn't handle any negative or sad news stories. I quoted scripture over and over again, "God has not given us a Spirit of fear but of a sound mind." "When I am afraid I will trust in Him." (is that scripture or just a song??) I battled, and I was determined to come out on top. Through this meditation on scripture and prayer, I did! I understood God with me in the Word, and his presence defeated the doubts.

There are times when that fear does creep back in, but I battle it down. I will not be motivated by fear. God doesn't want me to be fearful. He wants me to claim him in all circumstances and in all things because he will be victorious. He has already overcome the world, and I find comfort in that. God does still perform miracles; I've seen it. I can trust him for what is best for my family, even if I don't understand at the time.

My experiences have made me a better NICU nurse. I've been there. I've had almost every experience except for a baby dying in the NICU. I have always been a compassionate person, but I am more so now. I went through this so God would ultimately be glorified. My husband

and I can encourage and strengthen others in a way we could not before. Nothing replaces saying, "I've been there, and you can get through this, too." God uses challenging times to show his goodness and mercy, even if we don't understand the full picture.

Chapter 6
GOD'S LOVE IS PRESENT

Thereafter, Hagar used another name to refer to the LORD, who had spoken to her. She said, "You are the God who sees me." She also said, "Have I truly seen the One who sees me?"
Genesis 16:13 (NLT)

I REMEMBER VISITING THE CHAPLAIN'S office while attending Evangel University. I wanted answers. I wanted to know how God could be omniscient, omnipresent, omnipotent and full of love. I didn't see how it could all be true in light of my heartache. The campus pastor didn't have the answers for me, and he recommended I speak with someone from the theology department. What I needed then, and for many years afterwards, was not an intelligent explanation from a theologian. I needed to recognize God's presence and activity.

There are moments in life where it feels there is no way God is with us. We feel completely alone in our hurt, anger, or fear. The lie that God is not present can steal our hope. However, just as scripture had an abundance of examples to remind us of God's unfailing love, it is also full of the truth of his presence in our lives. You are not alone. You have never been, nor will you ever be, alone. God is with you.

We have already established God has an unchanging character. Therefore, we can jump straight into demonstrating God's present love throughout history. God was with mankind from the beginning, not as a distant observer, but as an active participant in the lives of humanity. He walked in the Garden of Eden (Genesis 3:8). When Adam and Eve's taste test of the forbidden fruit brought sin and death into the world, God put events in motion to bring man back into close, personal relationship with him. He did not leave man to his own devices. He was in control, and he was present.

God was always there. He made covenants with Abraham (Genesis 17); he guided Moses and the people of Israel with a pillar of cloud and a pillar of fire (Exodus 13); and his presence moved with the Ark of the Covenant (which was kept in the tabernacle) in the time of Israel's many kings (Exodus 30 and various Old Testament texts). Throughout the Old Testament, we see God was present and active. The individuals in these stories never knew the full picture of how their lives were part of fulfilling God's great plan to redeem mankind. They could only see their circumstances. Some lived without a single doubt of God's goodness and his perfect plan, and others, like the Israelites in the wilderness, would question God frequently. Our various responses to the trials of living are a natural part of the human experience.

God is not fazed by our fears and doubts, nor does he waiver in his persistent and present love for us. There is no comprehensible explanation for his love. His hand created the great expanse of the earth, yet he knows the very hairs on your head. Just like the people of Israel, we can't always see his plan and his presence. Nevertheless, his love never waivers and his purpose for us is good. The Old Testament God of presence did not change, he has always been with his people, no matter what the circumstances of the moment looked like.

Not only do we have examples of God's presence and activity, we see again and again that God promises to be with his people. For example, God spoke to Isaac as he was in the middle of a conflict with Abimelech. He reassured him of his presence and his promises: "'I am the God of your father, Abraham,' he said. 'Do not be afraid, for I am with you and will bless you. I will multiply your descendants, and they will become a great nation. I will do this because of my promise to Abraham, my servant'" (Genesis 26:24 NLT). We also see God assuring his people of his presence as he calls Moses to lead the Israelites out of captivity: "God answered, 'I will be with you. And this is your sign that I am the one who has sent you: When you have brought the people out of Egypt, you will worship God at this very mountain.'" (Exodus 3:12 NLT). Another example of the Old Testament promise of presence is found in Deuteronomy as Moses passes leadership of the Israelites to Joshua. Moses encourages the people by telling them what God has spoken to him, and he wraps it up with this encouragement, "So be strong and courageous! Do not be afraid and do not panic before them. For the LORD your God will personally go ahead of you. He will neither fail you nor abandon you" (Deuteronomy 31:6 NLT).

These promises of scripture were not just for the Old Testament followers of God. In Matthew 28:20, as Jesus is ascending to heaven he promises, "... And be sure of this: I am with you always, even to the end of the age." The promise extends to the end of time. We are part of this promise. Also, the writer of Hebrews cites the promise from Deuteronomy as a promise that continues beyond the time of Joshua: "Don't love money; be satisfied with what you have. For God has said, 'I will never fail you. I will never abandon you'" (Hebrews 13:5 NLT). The promise was understood by the New Testament audience, and should be understood today, as an eternal promise. We can rest assured God will never fail us or abandon us. Even when our circumstances feel out of control, he is with us.

This is obviously a very brief, simplified overview of God's constant presence and his promises for all time. Sometimes we forget the Bible is a great love story. My children's devotional, *The Jesus Storybook Bible* by Sally Lloyd-Jones, is a surprisingly beautiful explanation of the Bible. She demonstrates again and again how God was and is present and pursuing the hearts of men. I have purchased this book for many people because I cannot tell you the number of times the devotional ministered to me. I even used this children's devotional as the text for an adult Sunday school class. When I could not see through my own pain, the words from this book, "God loves you with a never ending, never giving up, unstopping, always and forever love," would bring tears to my eyes as I read to my children. I wanted so much for that to sink in and be truth in their lives despite the fact I struggled to believe it for myself. They were words my spirit knew to be truth, but I had struggled to reconcile my pain with them.

It was words like these from Sally Lloyd- Jones, and others like those of C.S. Lewis that kept me hanging on and would not allow me to fully let go of my faith. I was reminded of God's presence in my life through scripture, literature, and the relationships of Godly friends and family. The Holy Spirit reminded me again and again through these sources that God had not abandoned me.

If you are in a season of longing for God's love to be real in your life, I pray the stories and words in this book will keep you holding on and these words will be the message that speaks directly to the broken places with the truth God has not forgotten nor abandoned you. His love is present. His nature is demonstrated throughout history, and you are not excluded from the reach of his presence.

Life may not always make sense. We may not always receive the answers to the questions of "why?" We can know, though, that God is in control. The one who spoke the world into existence is also the one who has poured his presence out among us. A love from a God this big cannot be captured in a simple explanation. We cannot understand all the workings of the world because our God is not small enough for a human mind to explain and understand in every way. Although we serve a God our minds cannot tame, his presence can put our questions and our fears to rest. May the truth of his presence seep into the cracking and broken pieces of your heart, and may the Holy Spirit fill you with an ability to see how God was, is, and will continue to be with you.

PART 3

A DESPERATE NEED FOR GRACE

We can do our worst, but God's love is without condition.

Chapter 7

THE DAMAGE I
HAD DONE

When babies sleep before they wake,
I have no heart left to break.
And faith....
Nothing left to shake.

THE CHILDREN'S VOICES WERE RINGING with joy as they belted out Christmas songs. I stood there smiling sadly at my five year old daughter's performance as blood and a lost future were flowing out of me. As the performance came to a close, I kissed my son and two daughters and left them with my parents. My husband and I went to a hospital to undergo an ultrasound we already knew would show an empty womb. There is a strange imprint in my mind of the moments that passed as we left that hospital. Although we no longer live in the same city, I can still see the lights of a Pudgie's Pizza in a section of town as depressed as we were. We didn't eat dinner that night. Instead, we decided to put the day to bed. Although it was not anywhere near our normal schedule, we'd had our fill of that day. There was such a strange and acute sense of emptiness as we held each other and ached for what would never come to be. We were lost together.

....

I purchased a new diaper bag and some onesies in an act of faith. The test said positive, and I refused to live in fear that this would be another lost child. For further peace of mind, I scheduled an ultrasound at nine weeks. When the banter stopped during the exam, I knew I'd lost another baby. I was told to come back in a week to check again. For a full week I fluctuated between hope and despair. My husband and I struggled to understand each other's emotions during the waiting, so we floated alone next to each other in a sea of uncertainty. I had resigned myself to the loss before it was confirmed, and the disconnect between Jon and I grew. With the confirmation of the loss, we were separated from another baby, separated from the hope of life, and separated from each other.

Without a fight, Jon honored my request to go through the dilation and curettage procedure alone. My womb was clinically cleaned and emptied, and I felt the barrenness of my entire being.

....

I experienced a December miscarriage, the death of my cousin, Jalit, and her baby, Harley, in May, and another miscarriage in October. That less than one year window ended with the messy collision I referenced in the introduction- the bowling ball smashing into the pins. Yeah, that was me. The grief of loss upon loss and a need for perfection to prove my worth combined in a devastating blow. I had failed again to give my husband the larger family he desperately wanted, and the accumulation of deaths became more than I could bear. I wanted to escape the weight of the grief. I poured myself into my work; I cleaned the house with a new vigor; I cared for our children, and I ran miles and miles. I also did some things I could not explain nor understand.

In about a six month window, I went from one poor decision to the next, living with a complete lack of control. I couldn't stop myself. I released the grip I had held so tightly over my emotions, and an addiction I had not fully realized reared its ugly head. There is so much shame in all that occurred. Simply stated, I began by sexting a stranger I had met on the Words with Friends app, quickly moved to a long distance emotional/sexting affair with an old college flame, and bottomed out with a very brief sexual affair with a younger man in our church. I was not who I wanted to be. Here I was a pastor's wife, a mother of three, a respected teacher, and women's group leader, and I couldn't function anymore.

I had purchased the Bible I mentioned in the introduction of this book shortly after the long distance affair had come to a close. I felt farther from God than I ever had before, and I felt I did not deserve God's love. I was desperately in need of faith to believe his love could be for me. Although I was beginning to recognize the depth of my brokenness, I was too unstable at that point to find recovery from my addiction. It was not until the physical affair that I realized how out of control my actions really were.

When I realized I could not stop my behavior on my own, I scrambled to make a change to save my marriage. I scheduled a trip to visit my brother and get counseling with someone from his church. This led my husband to wonder what was happening. He knew I was feeling sad, but he had no idea how lost I was. He didn't understand why I was so desperate to get to a counselor. I didn't go on that trip. Instead, I told

Jon the damage I had done to our home, and I stayed to try to repair it. All growing up I had heard my parents say, "hurting people hurt people." I was definitely hurting, and I absolutely hurt people.

I found myself in a very difficult place. I was in desperate need of emotional healing, but I was also in a place where I needed to try to provide healing to someone else. I didn't have what it took to sustain myself, and now that my husband knew my need, he was too damaged by me to give me the emotional support I craved. He needed my emotional support because I had wounded him deeply, and I had nothing to give. For the first time in our marriage, divorce was on the table. We both needed God's love to repair our wounded hearts.

Although I had struggled to see God in my hurt and confusion, God was not absent from our lives. The love I desperately wanted, but felt I could no longer receive was active despite my struggle to see it. Prior to learning about my infidelity, Jon had felt impressed to study the book of Hosea. He didn't know why, and it didn't seem strange to him since Biblical study was such a common practice as he prepared sermons and wrote many graduate papers. Jon didn't know it, but he was doing a study because God was preparing him to love me the way God loves his people.

You see, the book of Hosea demonstrates a principle that has never changed: God has great mercy for those who seek forgiveness. His love looks beyond the consequences our actions deserve, and he pays the price for all to return to him. God was calling Jon to love me beyond what my actions deserved. We both needed to understand the book of Hosea- Jon to see how love can overcome betrayal, and me to see how love can exist for the betrayer.

Hosea is situated in the Old Testament, and in the Old Testament, the people understood God through the law. When the nation of Israel failed to obey the law, the consequences were severe: famine, death, and defeat at the hand of an enemy nation are a few examples of what would happen when God's people tried to separate themselves from God through their defiance and sin. The stepping outside of God's boundaries always had damaging effects.

In our times, the effects of sin are no less damaging. I had broken the trust of my husband, and the consequences my actions merited were a broken home. The pain extended down to my three children as they could hear mommy and daddy fighting at night. The security and stability they had always known was becoming uncertain. If God had not put it on Jon's heart to love the unfaithful, my children's lives would be drastically different because of my failing. The book of Hosea was an example our family desperately needed.

Hosea was a prophet called by God to marry a prostitute in order to demonstrate to the people of Israel how they had been unfaithful to God by worshipping other gods. Although Hosea's wife, Gomer, had three children with him, she was unfaithful to him. Hosea had every right to divorce Gomer and leave her to her own devices. However, God called Hosea to show Gomer grace and love:

> Then the LORD said to me, "Go and love your wife again, even though she commits adultery with another lover. This will illustrate that the LORD still loves Israel, even though the people have turned to other gods and love to worship them."
>
> So I bought her back for fifteen pieces of silver and a measure of wine. Then I said to her, "You must live in my house for many days and stop your prostitution. During this time, you will not have sexual relations with anyone, not even with me."
>
> This shows that Israel will go a long time without a king or prince, and without sacrifices, sacred pillars, priests, or even idols! But afterward the people will return and devote themselves to the LORD their God and to David's descendant, their king. In the last days, they will tremble in awe of the LORD and his goodness.
>
> Hosea 3 (CEV)

God's people had been unfaithful, and he used Hosea's life to serve as an example to the nation. God had been betrayed, and although he was justified in revenge and wrath, he chose to call his people back to him. Just as Hosea redeemed Gomer, God redeemed mankind. God's love was not and is not conditional on our actions.

The consequences of stepping outside of the boundaries God has placed for us are not simply spiritual. God places boundaries to protect us, and I saw my world unraveling as I jumped over the barriers God had put up for me. As I sought reprieve from my own pain, I found myself feeling more lost and confused than ever. I also caused great damage to my husband and my home. I was Gomer. I was Israel. I was unfaithful. I was undeserving of God's love.

There are many of us who can relate to Israel in the book of Hosea. Some, like me, because of blatant, obvious sin. Others of us have put our focus and energy on things that may not be innately bad, but when they are put before God, they can serve as idols in our lives. Once we stop putting God first, we can quickly find ourselves living in a world of blurred lines and crossing boundaries we never imagined approaching. Prior to my great failings, I could have turned to God to heal my heartache. Instead, I turned to the gods of exercise, work, and personal gratification. I was looking for anything to help me escape the pain. I had forgotten the greatest commandment and its purpose. When I turned my attention away from God, I felt the separation intensely. I remember texting someone during this time to ask if they believed God really holds us in his hands. I couldn't feel him holding me because I was busy chasing relief from things without the power to meet my need.

The Asbury Bible Commentary describes how the book of Hosea demonstrates God's relationship with a people who look to idols instead of him:

> The purpose of the book is to show a complacent Israel the true nature of their relationship with God and to call them back to the only One who truly loves them. He is the only One who can supply the very things for which they are petitioning their idols. The book is set up as a court case in which God, the aggrieved husband, brings charges against his faithless wife,

Israel (see 4:1-3). The charges include idolatry, sorcery, empty ritualism, corruption, faithlessness, brutality, and injustice. Nor are these merely the aberrations of a few; these conditions extend from the highest political and religious leaders right down to the dregs of society.

It would seem plain that nothing but divorce proceedings could issue from such horrendous failures. However, to the reader's surprise, that is not the case. Although the situation is dire, with all-but-inevitable consequences just ahead, still God does not want to dissolve his relationship with his beloved. Moreover, with prompt action, even those awful consequences could be averted. But if they are not, the coming disasters are not to be interpreted as expressions of God's abandonment of his people. Rather, they should be taken as spurs to return to the only One who ever really loved them.

After I had made a mess of everything, I called out to God wondering if he could show up for me despite my unfaithfulness. Just as Hosea did not divorce Gomer, and God did not leave the people of Israel, God continued to love me unconditionally. He demonstrated this through the people around me.

God had already put it in Jon's heart to show me the love I needed. God called Jon to lay down his right to leave me to my own devices. I was truly sorry for my actions, and I desperately wanted to be in relationship with God and with Jon. Jon's ability to love me in the midst of the great heartache I had caused him amazes me still to this day. Jon's love for me during that time is a tangible reminder to me of God's unfailing love for all, including me.

On the path to restoration, Jon and I fought and prayed. We went to counseling, and we fought. We prayed, and we fought. We made progress, and we fought... Eventually, we realized we were fighting for each other. We were giving everything we had to be present and to be in relationship. Spiritually, I was asking God for his help, but I wasn't even thinking about how to repair my relationship with him yet. I just knew I needed him to be a priority in my life because he was the only one big enough to restore our broken home. Not only did he restore our home, he redeemed our story. This broken, messy part of our story plays a major role in how we ended up where we are today. Although we took a painful path to get here, I have no doubt we are exactly where he wants us.

My infidelity caused us to move from our home in a small town in central New York to Northern Virginia. Before we left, we shared our heartache and my failings with many of our friends from the church where Jon was serving as a youth pastor and I was leading a women's Sunday school class. The response of other believers played a part in God wooing me. God used those around me to demonstrate what his grace looks like. Jon continued to love me when I did not deserve it, and others did the same. Our families recognized my sorrow and remorse, and they did all they could to help us heal. Those in the church who could have rejected me embraced me. Our friends and family rushed to surround *both* Jon and I with love and support.

After we came through the worst of it, I began to read the Bible I mentioned in the introduction to this book. I was ready to find the faith to believe that God's love was for me. I had seen it demonstrated, and I was ready to accept it. I soon found that it had been there all along. God had never forgotten me or left my side; when I was seeking refuge outside of him, he was preparing Jon and others to show me there is nothing I can do that is bad enough to stop him from loving me.

God has not turned his back on you. It does not matter what you have done. You can never reach a point where He will not accept you. He loves you with an unfailing, passionate, and pursuing love. His love will never quit; he will never choose another love over your love; and he will never tire of pursuing you- no matter how far you may wander or may run from him. There is nothing you can do that can cause God to love you any less or any more. He simply loves you.

God desires to be in relationship with you. He is constantly there, but he does not force you to love him in return. Instead, he faithfully waits with an undying love. When we feel the consequences of our actions, it is not because God has abandoned us; it is because we are being spurred to return to the one who loves us. We are unfaithful to God over and over in our lives, yet he forgives without limitations every time we ask. God's love is unconditional.

> *What, then, shall we say in response to these things? If God is for us, who can be against us? He who did not spare his own Son, but gave him up for us all—how will he not also, along with him, graciously give us all things? Who will bring any charge against those whom God has chosen? It is God who justifies. Who then is the one who condemns? No one. Christ Jesus who died—more than that, who was raised to life—is at the right hand of God and is also interceding for us. Who shall separate us from the love of Christ? Shall trouble or hardship or persecution or famine or nakedness or danger or sword? As it is written:*
> *"For your sake we face death all day long;*
> *we are considered as sheep to be slaughtered."*
> *No, in all these things we are more than conquerors through him who loved us. For I am convinced that neither death nor life, neither angels nor demons, neither the present nor the future, nor any powers, neither height nor depth, nor anything else in all creation, will be able to separate us from the love of God that is in Christ Jesus our Lord.*
>
> *Romans 8:31-39 (CEV)*

<u>Your Voice</u>

Take some time to reflect on your own story.

If you are studying this as a group, please allow people room to keep their stories private if they so choose. Each person should only share as he or she feels comfortable. However, don't rush through the questions as some individuals may need more time to think and process their own stories.

As you share, be sure to be clear about what you would like to be kept among the group and what is okay for others to repeat.

1. Have you ever made a mistake (or multiple mistakes) that caused you to feel God's love could not apply to your life?

2. What are some tangible ways you feel God demonstrates his love to people? List as many as you can.

3. Do you recognize any of the things you (or others in the group) have listed in number two in your own life?

4. Do you believe that God loves **you** personally? Why or why not?

If you do not feel God loves you personally and you want to believe his love is for you, pray God will reveal his love to you in a tangible way. (If you are comfortable, ask other group members to pray for you as well.)

Chapter 8

TAMARA'S BROKEN HALLELUJAH

Shame told me there was no other way.
I carried true life within my womb,
But I was left carrying shame's empty child.

THIS IS TAMARA'S STORY:

I was walking alone into a clinic to end my pregnancy. I guess I technically wasn't alone. There were picketers shouting at me and people waving their Bible's in my face, quoting Scripture and calling me a murderer. I kept my head down and tried my best to ignore their yelling and name-calling. I was here to get my life back, and no one was going to stop me.

I was too far along to terminate my pregnancy at the free clinic near my college, so I had to come up with $500 and drive four hours to St. Louis. My best friend at the time was in love with me. Raising someone else's child with his soul-mate was just not what he had in mind for our happy ending, so he gladly loaned me the money and drove the distance. I made some empty promises and gladly accepted his offer to help.

The man whose baby I was carrying had promised me the world. I fell in love with him before I knew he was married and had children, but even then that didn't stop me. I was too far gone at that point anyways. I lost my virginity at fifteen and had already slept with countless losers by college, so what was one more. And, this guy was a tattoo artist, so if I played my cards right I could even get some free ink out of the deal!

The night I let him tattoo me was the night I let him take me home. It was the first night I had ever let a married man do unspeakable and shameful things to my body in a bed he shared with his wife. It was me at an all-time new low. It was the night a seed was planted and the night that would change my life forever.

Needless to say, several months later I knew something was wrong. I couldn't smoke cigarettes without throwing up, my breasts were tender, and I felt hormonally out of control. I took a stolen pregnancy test alone in a K-mart bathroom and confirmed my worst nightmare. I was pregnant.

I immediately went to the tattoo parlor, but was only greeted by his business partner, and I was told that the father of my child had moved his family back to California. No goodbye. No anything. He knew what he had done, and that was that.

I couldn't just call my parents and ask for advice. I mean, I was a preacher's kid and to call my freshman year and announce that I was pregnant was just not something I could EVER do. It would ruin them, and it would completely screw up the path that I was on. I had to end it, and I had to end it fast.

So there I was in the heart of St. Louis, sitting on the table waiting for the doctor to come in and terminate my three month pregnancy. I was counseled before I went into the procedure room not to let it bother me; abortion was a normal and healthy option. I was trying to stay strong, but I knew deep down in my heart God was grieving at that moment. He was heartbroken over who his daughter had become and for the life that was being taken that day.

The pain was overwhelming as they tugged, pulled, and sucked the life out of me. The darkness in that room was thick and tangible, and I felt more alone than I ever had. I looked over my side and saw my lifeless baby squished up in a jar. The new life that was once inside of me was now inside glass and waiting to be disposed of like trash. That moment wrecked me. I began to weep because I knew how wrong I was. I knew I had just made the worst decision of my entire life.

As days and months passed, I tried to pick myself up and go on with life as usual. I attempted to get my life right with God, make Christian friends, and find a church I could call home, but the shame and the guilt was all consuming. Depression filled me to the very core, and my lack of self-worth eventually began my downward spiral into more horrible life choices.

I began drinking heavily and experimenting with drugs. I would often times drink so much I would black out and not even know how I had gotten home. I would sleep with any man who would buy me my next twelve-pack or get me high. I was obviously completely out of my mind and vulnerable most nights, which led to being taken advantage of by complete strangers and waking up cold, naked and ashamed. I was reduced to nothing. I had no part of my heart left to give anyone, especially not God.

One night, I was wasted and my friends let me drive home. On the way, I drove my car into a ditch. As I pulled into my Christian college campus that night, I was literally dragging pieces of metal behind my vehicle and had blood streaming down my face. The security guard at the gates stopped me, took one look at my face, and told me I needed Jesus. He said instead of turning me in, he was going to pray for me. You see, God had me the whole time. He had a plan, a redemption story, and it wasn't for me to die or get kicked out of college and move back home. The best was yet to come!

Over the next year I continued to make some pretty dumb choices, but I also felt a stirring in my heart. There was a longing for something more that wasn't there before. The Spiritual truths that were ingrained in me as a child began to show themselves, and the Holy Spirit began to bring conviction for my actions.

I was a liar, a whore, a cheat, a thief, an adulteress, and a murderer, and where that was once okay, suddenly I wanted more for my life. But how could I ever live a life of normalcy and allow myself to be loved by one man only? How could I ever be with one person in a healthy relationship for the rest of my life and be satisfied? Would I have to settle for status quo and live with someone I didn't love fully? Could any man even love me knowing the disgusting things I had done? In my mind, I envisioned the worst in my future husband, but my amazing God already had my life mate picked out. He was greater than anything I could ever have hoped for or imagined!

He began pursuing me. He knew my class schedule and would strategically place himself outside the building just as I was walking out. He would ask me how I was doing and seem genuinely interested in my life, and he eventually asked me out.

We have been married now for ten blissful years! God has given me a love for my man I never thought was possible, and there hasn't been a day I have been bored or dissatisfied with my life with him. He treats me like a queen and looks for new ways to serve me on a daily basis. I am a youth pastor's wife and am blessed to walk alongside this mighty man of God as we serve together in ministry, pouring into the lives of teenagers who desperately need a voice of hope.

In spite of the horrific day in St Louis, the Lord blessed us with three beautiful, healthy babies. In spite of what I deserved, I had the easiest, most uncomplicated pregnancies. Those children have radically changed my life. They have driven out the selfishness and the self-centered destructive ways that used to control my life, and every day I thank Jesus for them.

We serve an awesome God: a God who loves us in spite of our filth, a God who pursues us into right relationship with him, a God willing to overlook our past and redeem our future, and a God who blesses us mightily beyond what we deserve. His grace and mercy are new EVERY morning, and I pray all can know his unconditional love like I have, without having to walk through the fire.

Tamara's Voice

1. **Have you ever made a mistake (or multiple mistakes) that caused you to feel unworthy of God's love?**

    My life from the age of fifteen to twenty-two was nothing but one horribly painful mistake after the other. Each one, whether it was something stupid done in a drunken or drug-induced stupor or another man I let take full advantage of me, left me feeling dirty, disgusting, and completely unworthy of Christ's love and affection.

2. **What are some tangible ways you feel God demonstrates his love to people.**

    Obviously the biggest demonstration was his willingness to step out of Heaven, take on flesh, and bear a cross not his own for MY sin. But He's also there to embrace us in our weakest and broken moments of complete desperation. We are never too dirty for Him to wrap His loving arms around us and whisper those sweet words of truth into our ears.

    He lavishes great gifts on his children who are often times so unworthy. He chooses to bless us in spite of our unfaithfulness and selfish desires. He's a very perfect and gracious God, and for that I am forever grateful.

3. **Do you recognize any of the things you (or others in the group) have listed in number two in your own life?**

    From the moment I surrendered my life fully to Christ at the age of twenty-two, He has lavishly poured out his love towards me. He has blessed me with a husband who treats me like a queen, and he's given me three healthy children who have radically changed my life. He's placed us in a position of leadership where we are able to pour into and disciple young lives in the hopes that they don't have to walk through what we did as teenagers and young adults. He has blessed us financially in times when we could see no way out, and we have lacked for nothing. He has been faithful beyond our wildest dreams and imaginations.

4. Do you believe that God loves you personally? Why or why not?

I believe without a shadow of a doubt that God loves me. He has kept me and seen me through the darkest of hours, all the while watching and waiting for me to come back to Him, and when I did He welcomed me with open arms, and he redeemed ALL of me. He put my broken pieces back together and made me new. He made me feel worthy, special, and adored. Although I've stumbled, and my life hasn't been perfect since surrendering to Him, there is no longer the lingering and overwhelming feeling of guilt and unworthiness. Those feelings are now replaced with the understanding that I am not perfect, but I am forgiven.

Chapter 9

GOD'S UNCONDITIONAL LOVE

Therefore, there is now no condemnation for those who are in Christ Jesus, because through Christ Jesus the law of the Spirit who gives life has set you free from the law of sin and death. For what the law was powerless to do because it was weakened by the flesh, God did by sending his own Son in the likeness of sinful flesh to be a sin offering. And so he condemned sin in the flesh, in order that the righteous requirement of the law might be fully met in us, who do not live according to the flesh but according to the Spirit.

Romans 8:1-4 (CEV)

SHAME AND REGRET ARE POWERFUL forces. They can trap people into feeling their mistakes can never be overcome. Our mistakes often come with consequences- lost jobs, broken relationships, maybe even jail time. However, we tend to add to our own consequences. We suppose we cannot be forgiven or we cannot be loved. We allow our mistakes to keep us from pushing forward because deep down we believe ourselves to be unworthy of love and forgiveness. However, God's love isn't concerned with what our actions deserve because his love breaks the law of sin and death.

The law of sin and death is that all sin leads to death. However, we are not under the law of sin and death if we live in the victory Christ has provided. Romans 8: 1-2 says, "So now there is no condemnation for those who belong to Christ Jesus. And because you belong to him, the power of the life-giving Spirit has freed you from the power of sin that leads to death" (NLT). It doesn't say there is no condemnation for those who have lived a perfect life. When we accept Christ as the sacrifice for our mistakes and give him the primary role in our lives, there is freedom. We are no longer bound by our failures. We are no longer slaves to addictions and flaws; we have been "freed" by the power of the "life-giving Spirit." The requirement on our lives is not perfection; it is surrender. It is letting go of the sin and the shame in order to embrace God's love for us.

Almost everyone has heard the verse, "For this is how God loved the world: He gave his one and only Son, so that everyone who believes in him will not perish but have eternal life" (John 3:16 NLT). This verse is explaining the reason behind the action done to free us from the effects of sin. It is freedom from the grave, freedom from spiritual death, and freedom from the death of our God given dreams. When we live believing we are forever disconnected from God because of failings, we live in the law of sin and death. We forfeit the work of love that was done for us, and we are missing out on God's calling for our lives. His love and his plans are not hindered by the fact we are sinners.

I love the section in Matthew where the Pharisees were upset with Jesus for having dinner with tax collectors and "other disreputable sinners." Chapter 9 verse 13 says, "Then he added, "Now go and learn the meaning of this Scripture: 'I want you to show mercy, not offer sacrifices.' For I have come to call not those who think they are righteous, but those who know they are sinners.'" Jesus telling them they need to learn the meaning of a particular passage of scripture was a slap in the face because Pharisees were considered the residing experts of all things scripture related, and they considered themselves to be righteous because of their strict adherence to the laws of scripture. Jesus was turning everything upside down in the culture of that day. At that time, only those who lived strictly by the law were understood to be worthy of God. Yet, Jesus was telling them that he, God's son, was there specifically for those who were fully aware of their failings.

The law was not intended to separate man from God; it was there to allow him to come closer. God always provided a way for sin to be forgiven, and he never meant for us to hold onto guilt and shame. The Old Testament laws were meant to help people live full healthy lives, not to be used to exclude those who fall short. Even the law made provision for those who failed; and, when the time was right, God sent Jesus to be that provision for all time. People had twisted God's message to man, but Jesus came to set the record straight. He was the ultimate example of the grace and love God offers to those who fall short and fail to live within the healthy boundaries provided to us.

When the Pharisees tried to trap Jesus by asking him what the most important law was, Jesus boiled all the commandments down to two: "'You must love the LORD your God with all your heart, all your soul, and all your mind.' This is the first and greatest commandment. A second is equally important: 'Love your neighbor as yourself.' The entire law and all the demands of the prophets are based on these two commandments" (Matthew 22:37-40 NLT). Jesus was demonstrating the point that God is not asking us to never make mistakes. He is asking us to put him first. There are no hoops to jump through, there is no requirement for perfection. All the laws depended on those two because they were all built on God's love for us. Just as a parent sets boundaries for a child, God gave man rules to protect him from the deadly effects of sin. The law was given in love, and the love doesn't stop when we fail to follow the law.

God's love is for you. Your imperfections and failings do not disqualify you from his promises or his presence. He asks for you to love him in return and allow him to love others through you. He is not done with you just because you have caused great brokenness. He has a plan and purpose for all of who you are.

David, an Old Testament king, understood God's great love and great forgiveness for those who do not deserve it. He had an affair with Bathsheba, and had her husband sent to the front lines of battle so he would be killed. He repented, and he knew what it was to be loved by an unconditional love. In Psalm 103:7-12, David declares God's nature: "He revealed his character to Moses and his deeds to the people of Israel. The LORD is compassionate and merciful, slow to get angry and filled with unfailing love. He will not constantly accuse us, nor remain angry forever. He does not punish us for all our sins; he does not deal harshly with us as we deserve. For his unfailing love toward those who fear him is as great as the height of the heavens above the earth. He has removed our sins as far as the east is from the west" (NLT). This section of scripture depicts God's great love for humanity regardless of our failings. His love does not remove the sinner from his reach; it removes the sin. There is nothing we can do that can stop God's unfailing love because it is unconditional.

We all fall down, and we all make mistakes, but God's love for us is not dependent on our actions. He has demonstrated his desire for us to live in freedom and forgiveness. Jesus spent his time teaching against the condemnation we had taken on ourselves through the law. He taught about a father embracing the prodigal son, a shepherd pursuing the lost sheep, the woman seeking the lost coin, and master giving equal wages to all those who worked for him, regardless of the time of day they began the work. Each story was a picture of God seeking, embracing, forgiving, and blessing all people with equal love. There is no distinction or qualification of a need for perfection.

It took me some time to fully understand how deeply God loved me despite my failings, and even after I had embraced God's love for me, I worried my ability to speak to others about God would be hurt because of the mistakes I had made. I thought I would not have credibility as someone able to call others to leave the destruction of sin behind to pursue a pure life. People knew I was a Christian, and they saw me fail in a big way. I was convinced they would say, "She has no right to speak of how to be a follower of God. Look at what she did." However, God spoke to my heart about the fact his love is not contingent on my ability to be perfect. His love is perfect, and my imperfections only serve to demonstrate his love all the more. Those who know my past do not question my ability to speak about a need to follow God; it only serves to demonstrate all the more his great mercy and grace for even the worst of sinners.

WHAT GOOD IS A BROKEN HALLELUJAH?

Chapter 10

GOD'S LOVE REDEEMS THE BROKENNESS

Full Definition of Redeem

transitive verb

1a : to buy back : repurchase b : to get or win back

*2: to free from what distresses or harms: asa : to free from
captivity by payment of ransom b : to extricate from or help
to overcome something detrimental c : to release from blame
or debt : clear d : to free from the consequences of sin*

3: to change for the better : reform

4: repair, restore

*5a : to free from a lien by payment of an amount secured thereby
b (1) : to remove the obligation of by payment <the United States
Treasury redeems savings bonds on demand> (2) : to exchange for
something of value <redeem trading stamps>c : to make good : fulfill*

*6a : to atone for : expiate <redeem an error>b (1) : to offset
the bad effect of (2) : to make worthwhile : retrieve*

-http://www.merriam-webster.com/dictionary/redeem

ALL ALONG, WHEN I WAS breaking-being used, losing loved ones, and failing, God was active and involved. It was the breaking that taught me about unfailing, present, and unconditional love, and it was through the breaking I learned how to give and receive grace. God redeemed my life, and I could not truly understand what great worth I had been given without knowing guilt, shame, fear, and heartache.

When we left Central New York, it was because we needed a fresh start after the damages I had caused in our home. I was so very broken, and my brokenness had done great harm to my family. We uprooted our children from all they had known and moved to Virginia. I left my home town feeling torn and muddy.

When I first walked into the Bridge Community Church in Warrenton, VA, I was so relieved to be at a church where I was not married to staff. I was not the pastor's wife. I was just the woman who came, cried through most of the worship service, and left. It was during this time I began to see the worth of the broken pieces. I had already received unconditional love and grace from believers in New York who knew my story, C.S. Lewis's words describing Aslan's tears were knocking at my heart, and, as I read the Bible and prayed, the Holy Spirit helped me to see the nature of God's unchanging love. It was all coming together, and I was finally beginning to deeply understand God's unfailing, present, and unconditional love for me personally.

We needed our time at The Bridge Community Church in Warrenton, VA to heal. It was a three year season of balm for my soul. After a year there, knowing our story, Pastor Greg Hackett brought Jon on staff. It was in the ministry and life of the church God brought us to full restoration and called us to plant Redemption Church Charlottesville.

Several of the people from the church we left in New York live and serve with us here in Charlottesville, VA. We moved to Northern Virginia at the same time one couple moved to the Charlottesville area. Not long after, other couples from New York moved to the Charlottesville area also. We were being healed and equipped in Warrenton, and God was bringing a team to Charlottesville. These are the people who saw me in my worst moments, yet they have been some of the most active members in the church planting process with us. Their love and support have played a large role in developing our deep belief Christian faith should be lived authentically in community with generosity and grace. God has redeemed our story, and he is building a church with the pieces of our shattered moments.

This city is full of amazing churches that are doing great things for God. There is not a lack of dynamic churches filled with God's presence. We are here because new churches reach new people. God has brought our team together because he has a plan for those who have not yet connected to his unfailing, present, and unconditional love.

In many ways, my failures were the culmination of years of breakage. My broken moments were the catalysts necessary to move my family from New York to Virginia. Although we left because we needed a place to start over, God had bigger plans. God was writing a redemption story. He was taking the weakness, hurt, shame, and failures in my life and using them as he built Redemption Church- another place where people can come just as they are, but leave redeemed by a savior. God used all of who we were. Jon and I both had solid family upbringings, high levels of education, ample training, and determined personalities. Those things were all major parts of God preparing us to plant a church, but they were not the only pieces God used. Many people have told us that the authentic moments and our vulnerability in sharing our personal stories are what drew them back to the church atmosphere. God redeemed our broken moments in order to draw those who need to see God loves and uses broken lives too.

God is in the redeeming business. If you didn't read the definition of redeem at the beginning of the chapter, I highly recommend you go back to it. He is a God of transitive action. He transforms what others would consider damaged and worthless into treasures. Over time, I have come to understand the value of brokenness in the hands of a redeemer. My broken pieces have helped me to give more grace to those around me, pray with sincerity for those in need, and cry with those whom words could not console.

My husband has said one of the reasons he fell in love with me during college was I held him and cried with him when his grandfather died. I did not know Jon's grandfather, but I knew the pain he felt. I knew I had no words to heal him, but I did have a deep understanding of his pain, and that was exactly what he needed. I have cried in a dorm room with a friend as she told me about the relationships in her family being torn by deceit and betrayal; I have cried in a classroom with a student after I learned of the sexual abuse in her home; and I have cried at the altar with strangers whose exact needs I did not know but whose pain I could feel in my spirit. Those tears spoke volumes. Those tears said, "You are not alone. You are not forgotten. You are worth something. This damage does not isolate you and make you less of a person." I could not have cried those tears, if I did not live through the broken moments first.

Although I have come to understand God's great love for me in a new way. I still can feel the heartaches of the brokenness. I have asked God to heal me from the pain that clings to me like a damp blanket, yet I still bear the marks of a partially broken woman in my heart. I have experienced God's strength working in the lives of others through this pain on many occasions, but it was not until I prepared to share my story with others that I fully came to appreciate the beautiful asset brokenness is.

When we stop focusing on asking God to heal the brokenness and we accept God's grace in our lives, God uses our pain and weakness to do miraculous things. One Sunday, Pastor Greg Hackett of The Bridge Community Church talked about people as spiritual beings having a physical experience. He highlighted how we are a mixture of flesh, bones, and spirit. An understanding of this twofold property helps to reconcile the brokenness with the beauty. We are God's divine creation, and we are stamped with his image. The pain we experience is part of being flesh and bone. It is God's spirit in us that allows those moments of brokenness to be transformed into something beautiful.

As I mentioned earlier, it is easy to look at those moments when we were broken and question where on earth God was. We wonder why he didn't step in. I know you can agree when I say a little smack on the back of the head, maybe a flashing red stop sign, anything to stop me from some of my biggest mistakes, would have been nice! It also would have been nice if that miracle I prayed for had come to pass or if he had not stood by idle while I was innocent and helpless. We raise our hands, and we pound the air. We fluctuate between healing and hurt. We wonder why we still can feel stabs of pain, fear, or insecurity from our wounds. We may see the broken pieces of ourselves as deficiencies, as reasons we are of less value to God and others. However, they are some of the most valuable assets we possess.

In 2 Corinthians 12:7-10, notice where Paul's affliction comes from, what God tells Paul will suffice, and what makes Paul's weakness an asset.

> Therefore, in order to keep me from becoming conceited, I was given a thorn in my flesh, a messenger of Satan, to torment me. [8] Three times I pleaded with the Lord to take it away from me. [9] But he said to me, **"My grace is sufficient for you, for my power is made perfect in weakness."** Therefore I will boast all the more gladly about my weaknesses, so that Christ's power may rest on me. [10] That is why, for Christ's sake, I delight in weaknesses, in insults, in hardships, in persecutions, in difficulties. For when I am weak, then I am strong.
>
> 2 Corinthians 12:7-10 (NIV)

Paul tells us the thorn in his flesh was a messenger of Satan. Sometimes we forget we have a powerful enemy, and we want to blame God for the trials we face. However, you will also notice we have a God who is more powerful than our enemy. God tells Paul that the thorn in his side doesn't need to be removed because his grace is bigger than any affliction our enemy can put in our lives.

Finally, God tells Paul the weakness, the one that Satan sent to torment Paul, is what allows God's power to be made perfect in Paul's life. Yes, the very thing that was intended to torment and afflict and bring Paul low is the very thing God uses to make his power perfect in Paul's life.

Paul's pleading three times for the thorn in his flesh to be removed mirrors Jesus's prayers prior to his crucifixion. Jesus prayed three times that his cup of suffering would be removed, and then he accepted the suffering as a means to bring victory over the chains that began with man's initial fall. Jesus made himself weak by taking on our sins and the penalty of death. It was only his brokenness that had the power to heal the damage of man pulling himself away from God. Satan thought he had found a way to break man and crush our relationship with God by tempting Eve to fail in the garden and bringing pain and death, but God used those very things to show mankind just how far he is willing to go to be with us.

He could have stopped Adam and Eve from eating the fruit in the garden and saved man from the pain and suffering caused by being outside of his presence. However, God knew his grace would be sufficient. He knew man's weakness would allow for his strength to be perfect. God did not turn from man in his weakness, instead, he allowed himself to become a broken man in order to overcome the death and damages of sin.

You may have asked God to heal your brokenness, or felt abandoned by God because he did not stop the initial damage from occurring. This lie we buy, that God abandoned us in our times of need, only furthers the notion we are somehow lacking in worth. This is a lie meant to drive us farther from God and to hold us back from operating in the power that comes in our weak moments. In the light of Paul's revelation, we can be confident that although God may not have set the events in motion that broke us, he most definitely is not going to allow our brokenness to go unused.

God will use your broken pieces. You are valuable and beautiful in his sight. He has not abandoned you. He is not blind to your hurt and broken places. He became flesh and bone, and he understands being broken. Just as my brokenness has given me the gift to cry for the pain of others, do not think for a moment God has not grieved over the damages and the hurts of his children. I don't mean his children in a general sense; I mean you sitting right here with this book. You are the most precious individual in his eyes, and he did not look away or hide when you were losing everything. He was there, and he was filled with righteous anger at the injustice, and he was overcome with sorrow for your brokenness.

He is not a God to be overlooked; he is not a God who forgets the damages that have been done to his children. He is a God who takes what Satan meant for evil, and he turns it around to overcome the loneliness of a broken heart. God takes the broken pieces of our lives and puts them together to create people with the power to heal. He defeats the lies that are birthed in our moments of brokenness: the lies that we deserve to be alone, that we are undesirable and without value, and that we cannot be used. Those lies are defeated when we stop praying for the sting of our pain to be removed and accept the grace we are offered.

God reaches in and says, "MY GRACE is sufficient for you, for MY POWER is made perfect in weakness." If you accept his grace, and embrace the broken pieces rather than focusing on your desire for God to remove them, you will see him do mighty and miraculous things through what the devil meant to keep you weak.

You can sing hallelujah, not despite your brokenness, but because of your brokenness. It is the brokenness that allows you to be used fully. God's power is far greater than our strongest moments, and if we embrace the broken, we allow his power come through.

Chapter 11

KRISTI'S BROKEN HALLELUJAH

If life contains miracles, heaven forgot me. The accumulation of pain is too much, and I am ready to for to be over. All of it. I don't want to do this anymore. I am too broken. Period. The end.

THIS IS KRISTI'S STORY:

So, I have been doing some strength and conditioning training as of late. I wanted to participate in a Memorial Day Workout Fundraiser really badly. A few weeks prior to the event, I developed a pain in my knee. I did not want to let the pain keep me from participating, so I figured I would endure it. Except, I couldn't any longer, so I finally asked for help from a chiropractor, a massage therapist, and a trainer.

They could not determine what tightened up first, throwing my knee out of whack - ACL, quad, hamstring, adductor, whatever - I did not care where it originated, I just knew I was in excruciating pain and wanted it gone. You know the kind of pain that you cry out at night when switching positions in bed?

I did not tell anyone about my pain except my hubby and best friend. No one knew how much pain I was really in. I did not want anyone except those I trusted completely to know of my weakness. Nothing was going to stop me from being in that fundraiser. After utilizing all the helpers I mentioned earlier along with several LONG deep water runs - it loosened.

Just like that. Snap. Loose. Heaven.

If I had not tried to hide it and asked for help earlier, I would have found healing sooner. Lesson learned. But had I really learned that lesson? Had I really learned to ask for help and trust the process? No.

See, back in December, Christmas time to be exact, we were on vacation. I told my hubby, "I have lost all my faith. God has forgotten about me. I love you, and I don't want to hurt you. And trust me, I don't have the guts to do it myself, but I don't want to live anymore. The pain is too great, and I am so tired of hurting." Can you imagine my sweet, precious hubby having to hear those words? How do you respond to that? He said, "I wish you could see yourself through my eyes."

My heart was breaking and I, for several years, could not trust God. The fact was, I did not want to. I had been hurt by too many things - losing my grandparents, being abandoned by my father, self-abuse, addiction, rape, abortion, suicidal tendencies, depression, my mother dying, losing my family to broken relationships, financial struggle, being hurt while on missions by the church we served, a miscarriage, my mother-in-law dying, ENOUGH!

I was not going to trust anything ever again because I was not going to get hurt again. I am not sure why- why that night, why that place- but I asked for help. Help to trust again. I knew I needed God's help to teach me how to do that. I needed him to bring people into my life who could show me the way to that peace.

The next morning, we were at breakfast, and a girl sat down next to me. She had an oddly shaped tattoo behind her ear. I find tattoos fascinating! I don't have any, but I love the stories behind them- stories that are so important a person wants that memory forever with them. I also have this only child issue that causes me to think everyone wants to talk to me. So, I made small talk with her until a space opened in the conversation to ask about her tattoo. She said it was a semicolon, that she deals with depression and has suicidal thoughts, and that the semicolon represents an author choosing not to end a sentence, but continue it. She further explained the sentence was her life. She was the author and chose not to end it. A little much at 9 a.m. for me, but through my tears, I thanked her for sharing.

After returning home and carving out a lot of me time, starting a business that allowed me a creative outlet and expressions of self-love, I went to see my friend, Justin. He owns a gym in my hometown, and we've known each other forever. This is a story for another time, but a doctor told me there was no hope for "people like me" with a medical issue, and I refused to accept that. So I went to Justin and asked for help. Yeah, me, asked for help and trusted someone to help me. Stubborn as a mule, I swear, but even so, he was able to help me succeed.

A few months ago, I was at a vendor event for my business. This sweet, beautiful woman with kind eyes came up to my booth and chit chatted, took my card, said something about starting a church - yawn.

Well, she called me the next day and hired me for a Mother's Day event at said church (Redemption Church Charlottesville). I went to one of their services before the event to check out where I would be setting up and serving. Her husband was the pastor and giving the sermon. There was something wonderful in the message of the sermon.

Something about us not being here to judge or figure things out, that our only task on earth was to love. Plain and simple, love. Love those you agree with, love those whom you don't agree with - your only task is to love.

Ok, I thought, I'm down with that. But I am not joining another church - I will not be hurt or be a party to hurting again. Then again, I don't believe in coincidences. Conflicted. So the next week, I go and set up for the event. The sweet lady who hired me was preaching. She started her sermon with a blog post she wrote. From the first word of the message to the last, I was in tears. Hmmm... chalked it up to being an emotional day and the fact that I cry at EVERYTHING.

So, I went back. Then I went over to their house for a small group. Then I was learning about my spiritual gifts and joined the team. What was happening? What had I opened myself up to? I let them see me. Unworthy, messy, screwed up me. And, they still liked me. They likened the church to a hospital, and that if no one was sick or hurting, then there was no point for the existence of it. I was falling in love with this precious community. I was... well... trusting them and allowing them to show me God's love through their kindness and striving to build authentic community.

Pastor Jon said in a sermon, that all the icky, ugly (ok, paraphrasing) things that we have gone through in life are to help someone else through exactly that. And, that we are here to be someone's miracle. Me? A miracle? I thought that was saved for Saints, not sinners. Wait... could these people be my miracles? At that point, instead of my knee... it was my heart that loosened.

Just like that. Snap. Loose. Heaven.

So here am I Lord, open, trusting, loving and ready to be someone's miracle.

Your Broken Hallelujah

Can we sing together now? If not, I'll keep singing for you. *Let's sing together, or not. Maybe the singing is **still** too hard because the pain is **just** too deep. The lyrics say what your heart longs to believe, and the songs we sing are the faith you desperately need. The world pushes and pulls you and drags you around. Your heart is trampled and aches at the sound. The melody feels false and true as you are torn in two. You want to believe, and you want Him to come through. So sit and listen while I sing for you. This is our song, and **some day you will sing too**.*

You HAVE NOW HEARD THE story of how I came to sing a broken Hallelujah. We each have our own reasons that cause us to relate to the experiences of brokenness caused by others, the brokenness of being alive, or the brokenness we cause ourselves. It may be your own experiences or the experiences of someone close to you, but we share an understanding of what it is to break. I hope you have also come to understand God's unfailing, present, and unconditional love is for every individual, including those who hurt others, and including you.

My ability to sing along with the choruses of love and praise did not come overnight. Do not be discouraged if you are not all the way there yet. I cannot tell you how many times I stood and listened to the lyrics because my heart could not sing. It is my prayer these words will stay with you in the way Aslan's tears had captured me, the way the grace of others held me, and the way the scripture verses jumped from the screen to my heart.

I wrote my story for you. Now it is your turn. You have a beautiful story, a story worth telling. Our experiences may be very different from one another, but the principles of God's love and his ability to use all of who you are remain the same. Your story just might be the story someone else needs, but if you can't share your own, feel free to share mine.

About the Book

I hate to write this down. I hate to stare it in the face. I hate to look into the empty void and admit the pain -and admit the failures that follow. Part of me wishes you didn't need to hear it. I want to leave it alone. The problem is I just can't. I can't stop until it is all down in print. God won't let me. He has this thing he wants you to see, and I have to paint the picture for you, or I will always feel it pushing at me, nagging me to do it already: say what he wants me to say. So here is my prayer:

"God, sometimes I wish you would just me leave me alone, and then I am extremely grateful that You won't and You don't. Use me up so that I can be full."

-Excerpt from my thoughts and prayers journal.

SHORTLY AFTER GOD CALLED US to plant a church in Charlottesville, I felt impressed to write. The phrase, "a book to build a church on," came to me again and again. I did not know what to write, but I was willing. One Saturday, I woke up before everyone else in the house, and all the kids actually stayed asleep. I felt prompted to write. The words I began with that day came flowing out and became the introduction and the framework of this book.

Because I have felt this book is something God called me to write as, "a book to build a church on," I have dedicated to give a reverse tithe- 90% of any money I earn from the sale of this book goes to Redemption Church Charlottesville and 10% will go to me. I am not sure if the phrase was meant to be taken as a physical building of the church through financial provision or if it was meant to be understood as a book to build up the people of the church. Either way, the book is written, and God can use it however he likes!

If you would like to know more about the church this book is written for, you can visit our website at redemptioncc.com. We are also on Facebook as Redemption Church Charlottesville.

About the Author

Rebecca is a lover of God, a wife, a mother to three, an avid runner, a chai tea drinker, and a recovering perfectionist. She has found great joy in owning her flaws and learning to rely on God and his great grace.

In her professional life, Rebecca has had the honor of working with middle and high school students for over twelve years. She graduated with top honors from Evangel University in Springfield, MO with a BA in Spanish Education and English. She also holds an MA in English from the State University of New York at Cortland. Rebecca has been published in educational journals, presented at various forums, and received local and national recognition in the educational field. Presently, she teaches English at Albemarle High School.

One of Rebecca's greatest passions is the ministry she and her husband are developing as the planting pastors of Redemption Church Charlottesville, an Assemblies of God church located in Central Virginia. They have a heart to see people connect to God's redeeming power through community, authenticity, generosity, and grace.

Rebecca enjoys ministering in small groups, at women's events, and for full congregations. Her dream is to make writing and speaking her full time career. Currently, she blogs at rebecaburtram.com, contributes to tworiversblog.com, and is the editor for the Church Multiplication Network's CMN Wives Blog.

Study Plans

*Videos can be found at rebeccaburtram.com

I am so excited you have chosen to use this book as a group study. I pray God will help you to encounter a deeper understanding of the unfailing, present, and unconditional nature of his love as you share in community. I am fully convinced we were created to be in community. On more than one occasion I have said, "There is something healing in the sharing. We need to let people into our lives because shared experience is a mathematical phenomenon: the weight of grief is divided and the celebration of joy is multiplied. Life was meant to be lived together." That is a huge part of what has motivated me to share my own story.

I am providing some suggestions for using this book as a group study. However, each group is different, and you will need to consider the needs of your particular group. The suggestions are set for an hour long session. Feel free to alter the study guides however you would like to meet the specific needs of your group. A few general notes before getting into the specific plans:

1. This study may cause people to deal with some big issues in their lives of which you may not be aware. I ask you to enter into each group meeting with prayer and to be sensitive to one another.

2. Because some of the information may include events that are not our proudest moments, be sure everyone is clear about what is okay for people outside the group to know and what is not.

Do not break confidence unless someone is harming themselves or others. (In this case contact the proper authorities only.) Also, please give room for people to share or to not share during discussion times. Some people will be eager to share, and others will need a little wait time before they open up. Don't rush through the questions.

3. The purpose of the group study is to grow together. It is not an opportunity to judge others or tell them how to live their lives. Please be sensitive to the guidance of the Holy Spirit. Sometimes, the best thing you can do is listen and indicate you understand. Pray for and love each other. Recommend a professional counselor if you really feel someone is in need of more than your love, support, and prayer.

4. Try to keep discussions from being focused on a single person. Some groups like to set a timer for each question. For example, if a timer were set for 10 minutes allotted to question 1, you may want to set a 2 minute time limit for each individual who is sharing. It is okay to allow for a quiet space between people sharing. You will be surprised by how many people may share if you wait for them.

5. Most importantly, keep the focus on God. There is a temptation to get bogged down in the messes being shared. Remember to focus on God's presence and love in the midst of the mess and his ability to use our broken lives.

5 or 6 Week Plan:

Week One:

1. (10-15 minutes) Open with prayer. Ask each participant to share his or her favorite worship song or hymn and whether or not it has special meaning. Encourage people to tell the story of what makes the song important to them. This allows new groups to get to know each other a little, and it gets established groups talking.

2. (15 minutes) Watch the author's online video and read the introduction out loud together.

3. (20-30 minutes) React to the material: Come up with your own questions, allow people to share freely in response to the content, or use some of these questions:
    a. What was your reaction to a pastor's kid/Christian college graduate/pastor's wife admitting to struggling in her faith? Surprise? Horror? A lack of surprise... as in, of course someone in those roles would struggle?
    b. What stood out to you most as you heard/read this section? Why?
    c. Do you agree with the author that life is hard? Why or why not?
    d. Have you ever found it difficult to enter into a worship song because the lyrics did not line up with your emotions/faith/etc.?

4. (3-5 minutes) Assign next week's reading. Participants should read all of Part 1 and answer the questions in their books. There are three chapters in Part 1. Each chapter will probably take less than 15 minutes to read.

5. (5-10 minutes) Close in prayer. Share requests. Pray for God to reveal his love in a fresh way to each group member.
    -You may also want to pray for others who come to mind

that might benefit from this study (then invite them to come to the next session).

Week Two:

1. (10-15 minutes) Open with prayer. Ask people to share their general reactions to the reading. How did they feel while reading? Was the amount of reading reasonable; did they have time to finish the reading? How did they feel about the questions they had to answer in their books?
2. (3-5 minutes) Watch the author's online video for Part 1.
3. (20-30 minutes) Use this time to go over the discussion questions from Part 1 of the book. Also, feel free to ask participants to react to thoughts, ideas, and stories from this section and how they related to them personally.
    a. Are there wounds in your life that have been caused by those close to you? If so, how has this impacted your view of God?
    b. What are some of the ways God has blessed you? Have any of those occurred while you were experiencing a time of heartache and pain?
    c. What are some of the dreams God has put on your heart? Tell about how you have seen God use painful circumstances to fulfill those dreams, or how the broken moments you are in now might be bringing you closer to fulfilling those dreams.
    d. What in particular stood out to you in this part of the book? Why?
4. (3-5 minutes) Assign next week's reading. Participants should read all of Part 2 and answer the questions in their books.
5. (5-10 minutes) Close in prayer. Share new requests and follow up on previous requests. Pray for God to reveal his love in a fresh way to each group member and for members to understand how to communicate God's love to those who have broken pieces. Pray for healing of damages caused by others.

Week Three:

1. (10-15 minutes) Open with prayer. Ask people to share their general reactions to the reading.
2. (3-5 minutes) Watch the author's online video for Part 2.
3. (20-30 minutes) Use this time to go over the discussion questions from Part 2 of the book. Also, feel free to ask participants to react to thoughts, ideas, and stories from this section and how they related to them personally.
   a. Have there been painful experiences in your life that are simply the result of being alive (not caused by the actions of others or by your own actions)? If so, has this impacted your view of God?
   b. What are the things in life that reveal God's active presence in the world? (The intricacy of creation, the birth of a child, a miraculous work... be specific about the things that speak to you individually.)
   c. Does reflecting on God's active presence impact your perspective concerning God and the pain you have experienced? Do you see him in your situation, or do you see him as a distant observer?
   d. What in particular stood out to you in this part of the book? Why?
4. (3-5 minutes) Assign next week's reading. Participants should read all of Part 3 and answer the questions in their books.
5. (5-10 minutes) Close in prayer. Share new requests and follow up on previous requests. Pray for God to reveal his love in a fresh way to each group member and for members to understand how to communicate God's love to those who have broken pieces. Pray for healing for the hurts that come from natural causes.

Week Four:

1. (10-15 minutes) Open with prayer. Ask people to share their general reactions to the reading.

2. (3-5 minutes) Watch the author's online video for Part 3.

3. (20-30 minutes) Use this time to go over the discussion questions from Part 3 of the book. Also, feel free to ask participants to react to thoughts, ideas, and stories from this section and how they related to them personally.

    a. Have you ever made a mistake (or multiple mistakes) that caused you to feel God's love could not apply to your life?

    b. What are some tangible ways you feel God demonstrates his love to people? List as many as you can.

    c. Do you recognize any of the things you (or others in the group) have listed in number two in your own life?

    d. Do you believe that God loves **you** personally? Why or why not?

    e. What in particular stood out to you in this part of the book? Why?

4. (3-5 minutes) Assign next week's reading. Participants should read the conclusion. If your group is participating in a 5 week study, the section "Your Broken Hallelujah" should also be read this week.

5. (5-10 minutes) Close in prayer. Share new requests and follow up on previous requests. Pray for God to reveal his love in a fresh way to each group member and for members to understand how to communicate God's love to those who have broken pieces. Pray for healing for the hurts that come from the damages we cause.

Week Five:

1. (10-15 minutes) Open with prayer. Ask people to share their general reactions to the reading.

2. (3-5 minutes) Watch the author's online video for the conclusion.

3. (20-30 minutes) Use this time to react to the conclusion (and "Your Broken Hallelujah" if this is your final week). Here are some possible discussion questions, but feel free to use your own.

    a.   Do you (or have you) viewed the broken areas of your life as hindrances to being able to serve God?

    b.   Have your broken areas helped you to relate to others?

    c.   What good is your broken hallelujah?

    d.   What in particular stood out to you in this part of the book? Why?

4.   (3-5 minutes) If this is a six week session, assign next week's reading. Participants should read the section "Your Broken Hallelujah."

5.   (5-10 minutes) Close in prayer. Share new requests and follow up on previous requests. Pray for God to reveal his love in a fresh way to each group member and for members to understand how to communicate God's love to those who have broken pieces. Pray for God to reveal the value of our broken hallelujahs to each of us individually.

Week Six:

1.   (10-15 minutes) Open with prayer. Ask people to share their general reactions to the reading.

2.   (15-20 minutes) Talk briefly about the final section, "Your Broken Hallelujah." Challenge each participant to write some of their own story down, and provide about 15 minutes of quiet time for them to do so. I recommend providing participants with paper and something to write with. I also suggest playing some worship music as participants write.

3.   (15-20 minutes) Take some time to allow participants to share portions of their writing, thoughts they had while writing, or other discussion topics related to the study and the activity.

4.   (5-10 minutes) Pray that God will give you each a voice to sing your own hallelujah, however broken it may be.

10 Week Plan:

Week One:

1. (10-15 minutes) Open with prayer. Ask each participant to share his or her favorite worship song or hymn and whether or not it has special meaning. Encourage people to tell the story of what makes the song important to them. This allows new groups to get to know each other a little, and it gets established groups talking.

2. (15 minutes) Watch the author's online video and read the introduction out loud together.

3. (20-30 minutes) React to the material: Come up with your own questions, allow people to share freely in response to the content, or use some of these questions:
   a. What was your reaction to a pastor's kid/christian college graduate/pastor's wife admitting to struggling in her faith? Surprise? Horror? A lack of surprise... as in "of course" someone in those roles would struggle?
   b. What stood out to you most as you heard/read this section? Why?
   c. Do you agree with the author that life is hard? Why or why not?
   d. Have you ever found it difficult to enter into a worship song because the lyrics did not line up with your emotions/faith/etc.?

4. (3-5 minutes) Assign next week's reading. Participants should read Chapter 1 and answer the "Your Voice" questions in their books.

5. (5-10 minutes) Close in prayer. Share requests. Pray for God to reveal his love in a fresh way to each group member.

   -You may also want to pray for others who come to mind

that might benefit from this study (then invite them to come to the next session).

Week Two:

1. (10-15 minutes) Open with prayer. Ask people to share their general reactions to the reading. How did they feel while reading? Was the amount of reading reasonable; did they have time to finish the reading? How did they feel about the questions they had to answer in their books?

2. (20-30 minutes) Use this time to go over the discussion questions from Chapter 1. Also, feel free to ask participants to react to thoughts, ideas, and stories from this chapter.

    a. Are there wounds in your life that have been caused by those close to you? If so, how has this impacted your view of God?

    b. What are some of the ways God has blessed you? Have any of those occurred while you were experiencing a time of heartache and pain?

    c. What are some of the dreams God has put on your heart? Tell about how you have seen God use painful circumstances to fulfill those dreams, or how the broken moments you are in now might be bringing you closer to fulfilling those dreams.

    d. What in particular stood out to you in this part of the book? Why?

3. (3-5 minutes) Assign next week's reading. Participants should read Chapters 2 and 3.

4. (5-10 minutes) Close in prayer. Share new requests and follow up on previous requests. Pray for God to reveal his love in a fresh way to each group member and for members to understand how to communicate God's love to those who have broken pieces. Pray for healing of damages caused by others.

Week Three:

1. (10-15 minutes) Open with prayer. Ask people to share their general reactions to the reading.
2. (3-5 minutes) Watch the author's online video for Part 1.
3. (20-30 minutes) Use this time to react to thoughts, ideas, and stories from this section.
   a. Emma said, "I decided God was distant, uncaring, and did not hear me. I thought, *Why bother with Him*? I still believed and wanted to be saved, but I unconsciously kept Him at arm's length. I felt a God that allowed so much pain and oppression obviously did not care about me on a personal level." Have you ever felt as Emma did? What changed to help you understand God's love for you personally? What would you have told Emma if you had known her at that point in her life?
   b. How does the understanding of God's love as unfailing compare to understanding the love we see displayed by those in our lives or in the culture around us? Are there people in your life you wish God would not love with an unfailing love? What encouragement comes from knowing God loves even those people with an unfailing love?
   c. What in particular stood out to you in this part of the book? Why?
4. (3-5 minutes) Assign next week's reading. Participants should read Chapter 4 and answer the "Your Voice" questions in their books.
5. (5-10 minutes) (5-10 minutes) Close in prayer. Share new requests and follow up on previous requests. Pray for God to reveal his love in a fresh way to each group member and for members to understand how to communicate God's love to those who have broken pieces. Pray for healing of damages caused by others.

Week Four:

1. (10-15 minutes) Open with prayer. Ask people to share their general reactions to the reading.

2. (20-30 minutes) Use this time to go over the discussion questions from Chapter 4. Also, feel free to ask participants to react to thoughts, ideas, and stories from this section and how they related to them personally.

   a. Have there been painful experiences in your life that are simply the result of being alive (not caused by the actions of others or by your own actions)? If so, has this impacted your view of God?

   b. What are the things in life that reveal God's active presence in the world? (The intricacy of creation, the birth of a child, a miraculous work… be specific about the things that speak to you individually.)

   c. Does reflecting on God's active presence impact your perspective concerning God and the pain you have experienced? Do you see him in your situation, or do you see him as a distant observer?

   d. What in particular stood out to you in this part of the book? Why?

3. (3-5 minutes) Assign next week's reading. Participants should read Chapters 5 and 6.

4. (5-10 minutes) Close in prayer. Share new requests and follow up on previous requests. Pray for God to reveal his love in a fresh way to each group member and for members to understand how to communicate God's love to those who have broken pieces. Pray for healing for the hurts that come from natural causes.

Week Five:

1. (10-15 minutes) Open with prayer. Ask people to share their general reactions to the reading.

2. (3-5 minutes) Watch the author's online video for Part 2.

3. (20-30 minutes) Use this time to react to Chapters 5 and 6. Here are some possible discussion questions, but feel free to use your own.

   a. Brooke said, "These experiences made a crack in my faith. The fear and doubt had left place for Satan to creep in and plant more seeds of fear and doubt. I struggled for weeks. I was fearful to even leave the house. I cried in the shower asking God, why I felt so lost. Why didn't I feel like myself? Why was I so fearful? I lived fearful something was going to happen to me or my kids or my husband." Have you ever felt like your experiences made a crack in your faith that only seemed to grow? What might you have said to Brooke if you had known her during this time? What scriptures might speak to Brooke's situation?

   b. How does understanding God's continual presence and his promises help you to reconcile the hurts of living with your faith?

4. (3-5 minutes) Assign the reading for next week. Participants should read Chapter 7 and answer the "Your Voice" questions.

5. (5-10 minutes) Close in prayer. Share new requests and follow up on previous requests. Pray for God to reveal his love in a fresh way to each group member and for members to understand how to communicate God's love to those who have broken pieces. Pray for healing for the hurts that come from natural causes.

Week Six:

1. (10-15 minutes) Open with prayer. Ask people to share their general reactions to the reading.

2. (20-30 minutes) Use this time to go over the discussion questions from Chapter 7 of the book. Also, feel free to ask participants to react to thoughts, ideas, and stories from this chapter.

a. Have you ever made a mistake (or multiple mistakes) that caused you to feel God's love could not apply to your life?

b. What are some tangible ways you feel God demonstrates his love to people? List as many as you can.

c. Do you recognize any of the things you (or others in the group) have listed in number two in your own life?

d. Do you believe that God loves **you** personally? Why or why not?

e. What in particular stood out to you in this part of the book? Why?

3. (3-5 minutes) Assign next week's reading. Participants should read Chapters 8 and 9.

4. (5-10 minutes) Close in prayer. Share new requests and follow up on previous requests. Pray for God to reveal his love in a fresh way to each group member and for members to understand how to communicate God's love to those who have broken pieces. Pray for healing for the hurts that come from the damages we cause.

Week Seven:

1. (10-15 minutes) Open with prayer. Ask people to share their general reactions to the reading.

2. (3-5 minutes) Watch the author's online video for Part 3.

3. (20-30 minutes) Use this time react to thoughts, ideas, and stories from Chapters 8 and 9. Here are some possible questions:

a. Tamara says, "My life from the age of fifteen to twenty-two was nothing but one horribly painful mistake after the other. Each one, whether it was something stupid done in a drunken or drug-induced stupor or another man I let take full advantage of me, left me feeling dirty, disgusting, and completely unworthy of Christ's love and affection." What might you have said to Tamara if you had known her at this time? What scriptures might speak to her situation?

   b. What does unconditional love mean? What scripture from the reading resonated with you most? Why?

   c. What in particular stood out to you in this part of the book? Why?

4. (3-5 minutes) Assign next week's reading. Participants should read Chapter 10.

5. (5-10 minutes) Close in prayer. Share new requests and follow up on previous requests. Pray for God to reveal his love in a fresh way to each group member and for members to understand how to communicate God's love to those who have broken pieces. Pray for healing for the hurts that come from the damages we cause.

Week Eight:

1. (10-15 minutes) Open with prayer. Ask people to share their general reactions to the reading.

2. (20-30 minutes) Use this time react to thoughts, ideas, and stories from Chapter 10. Here are some possible questions:

   a. Do you (or have you) viewed the broken areas of your life as hindrances to being able to serve God?

   b. Have your broken areas helped you to relate to others?

   c. What value is there in a broken hallelujah?

   d. What in particular stood out to you in this part of the book? Why?

3. (3-5 minutes) Assign next week's reading. Participants should read Chapter 11.

4. (5-10 minutes) Close in prayer. Share new requests and follow up on previous requests. Pray for God to reveal his love in a fresh way to each group member and for members to understand how to communicate God's love to those who have broken pieces. Pray for God to reveal the value of our broken hallelujahs to each of us individually.

Week Nine:

1. (10-15 minutes) Open with prayer. Ask people to share their general reactions to the reading.
2. (20-30 minutes) Use this time react to thoughts, ideas, and stories from Chapter 11. Here are some possible questions:
   a. Kristi had experienced the brokenness from all three areas discussed in this book, and she was feeling as though she did not want to continue living. Have you ever felt this way? What might you have said to Kristi if you had known her at that time? What scriptures might apply to her situation?
   b. How did God demonstrate unfailing, present, and unconditional love in Kristi's story?
   c. How does Kristi's story demonstrate the value of the brokenness Rebecca experienced? How are the two stories tied together?
   d. What in particular stood out to you in this part of the book? Why?
3. (3-5 minutes) Assign next week's reading. Participants should read the section "Your Broken Hallelujah."
4. (5-10 minutes) Close in prayer. Share new requests and follow up on previous requests. Pray for God to reveal his love in a fresh way to each group member and for members to understand how to communicate God's love to those who have broken pieces. Pray for God to reveal the value of our broken hallelujahs to each of us individually.

Week Ten:

1. (10-15 minutes) Open with prayer. Ask people to share their general reactions to the reading.
2. (15-20 minutes) Talk briefly about the final section, "Your Broken Hallelujah." Challenge each participant to write some of their own story down, and provide about 15 minutes of quiet

time for them to do so. I recommend providing participants with paper and something to write with. I also suggest playing some worship music as participants write.

3. (15-20 minutes) Take some time to allow participants to share portions of their writing, thoughts they had while writing, or other discussion topics related to the study and the activity.

4. (5-10 minutes) Pray that God will give you each a voice to sing your own hallelujah, however broken it may be.